TRAIN TO CHANGE
PHASE ONE
SELF-MASTERY

A Self-Help Training Program for Transformation
Forged Over Forty Years of Army Service

Train to Change
Phase One: Self-Mastery

© 2026, by J. Reed Durand

Print ISBN: 979-8-9950418-3-2

Managing Change
2810 N Church St
PMB 175679
Wilmington, Delaware 19802

Disclaimer

Purpose of This Book

This book is for educational and self-development purposes only. It is not a source of medical, mental health, psychological, therapeutic, diagnostic, or spiritual advice. It does not diagnose, treat, cure, or prevent any condition. Readers should seek guidance from qualified, licensed professionals for any physical, mental, emotional, or spiritual concerns, or for any matter requiring professional judgment.

The self-assessments, exercises, and tools included here are general self-help resources meant to support reflection and self-awareness. They are not clinical, comprehensive, or definitive evaluations. Other tools may be more appropriate depending on individual needs, and readers are encouraged to explore additional methods and perspectives as their goals evolve.

Professional and Institutional Independence

This book draws on the author's forty years of service across two careers with the United States Army, including experience in leadership, personal development, and organizational change. The insights presented are solely the author's and do not represent the official views, policies, or endorsements of the Department of Defense, the Department of the Army, or any other government agency.

References to military organizations, processes, or experiences are provided for illustrative and educational purposes only. They should not be interpreted as official guidance, doctrine, or instruction.

Real-Life Experiences and Composite Characters

The scenarios in this book are based on real-life experiences gained through many years of leadership and organizational work. Unless specifically noted as personal stories or direct quotes, all characters are fictional composites developed by blending traits, behaviors, and situations from various sources to emphasize key lessons.

Any initials or genders assigned to these characters are fictional. Any resemblance to actual individuals, living or deceased, is purely coincidental. This approach protects confidentiality, preserves privacy, and keeps the focus on the underlying concepts rather than identifiable people.

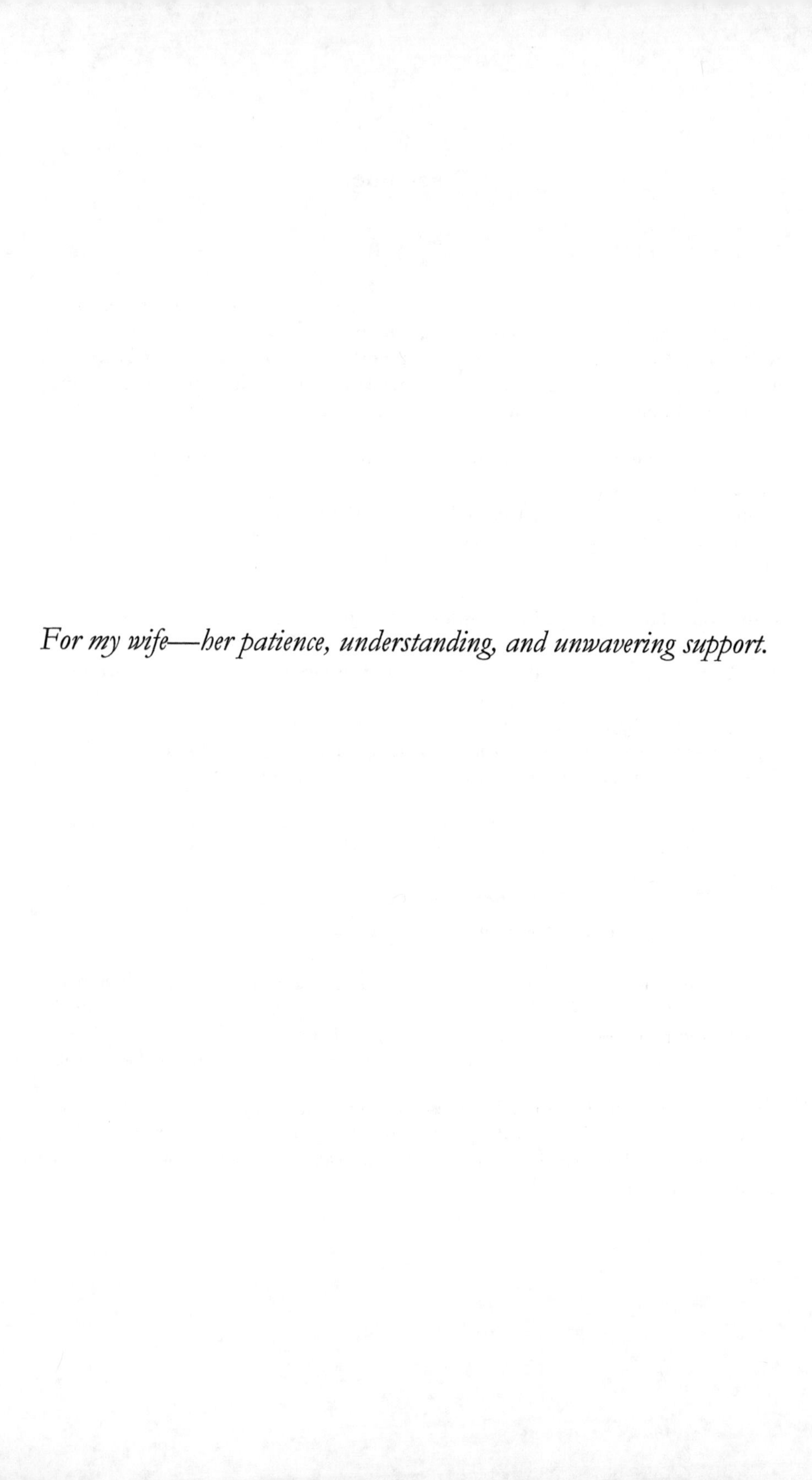

For my wife—her patience, understanding, and unwavering support.

Table of Contents

Preface

Managing change is a skill—something that can be learned, practiced, and mastered over a lifetime of personal and professional growth.

This book teaches you that skill.

Most of us have gone through the same frustrating cycle: we decide that this time things will be different—tomorrow, next week, next month, or next year. We genuinely commit to change, only to see old habits and routines quietly take back control. This isn't because we lack motivation, discipline, or willpower.

It's because few of us were ever taught *how* to manage change in our own lives.

Change isn't a mystery. Like any skill, it follows recognizable patterns. When those patterns are understood and practiced, achieving meaningful, lasting change becomes possible—not just once, but repeatedly across different areas of life.

This book series offers a practical, three-phase system to help you achieve that goal. The first book introduces Phase One, where all lasting change begins: within you.

Phase One focuses on two key parts of self-improvement:

Self-awareness: Knowing

Self-mastery: Doing

Self-awareness helps you see yourself clearly—your patterns, triggers, tendencies, and values—without judgment or harsh self-criticism. Self-mastery is the ability to act on that understanding—controlling your thoughts, aligning your choices with your values, and following through even when change feels uncomfortable.

Together, they establish the foundation for personal growth.

Many people struggle not because change is impossible, but because their inner world is divided. Doubt competes with their intentions. Impulse takes precedence over purpose. The real battle happens quietly within the mind—and winning that fight requires skill, not perfection.

I learned this early, in an environment where change was not optional. In the Army, adaptability and self-mastery were essential survival skills. Over time, I realized that change isn't something to just endure—it's something to accept, practice, and master. That insight shaped decades of work studying leadership, motivation, and transformation, not as abstract concepts, but as practical skills.

This book reflects that experience.

Inside, you'll find practical tools, exercises, and assessments designed to help you develop internal readiness for change. You'll also discover timeless insights—ideas that have guided human growth for thousands of years—combined with modern psychology and real-world application.

By the end of Phase One, you'll gain a clearer understanding of change. More importantly, you'll know yourself better. Most importantly, you'll begin to develop the skills to intentionally guide your life rather than just react to it.

This is more than just a self-help book. It's a manual for self-leadership training.

To be ready to change, you must first master yourself.

Let's Go!

Introduction

Everything is changing, all the time.

Learning Objectives. By the end of this introduction to Phase One, you will be able to:

1. Analyze three perspectives on planned personal change and apply them to your own journey.
2. Explain and apply the behavioral formula that influences your decision-making.
3. Assess your current stress level and prioritize actions to reduce it.

The world you knew yesterday no longer exists today, and it will have changed again tomorrow. Change is constant and unavoidable. How we respond to it shapes our lives, for better or worse.

It influences everything: the global economy, our national, state, and local socioeconomic realities, our workplaces, neighborhoods, families, political systems, and cultural norms. Whether we welcome it or resist it, act or react, change shapes our opportunities, challenges, and personal growth.

This training program is designed to help you achieve meaningful self-improvement. It emphasizes practical skills over theory, equipping you with the tools needed for effective planning and execution. You'll learn proven techniques that can lead to success, regardless of your current situation or background. These methods have been tested and proven over decades in real-world settings, including military environments and challenging personal and organizational circumstances.

In summary, what you'll learn here works.

You can count on it to guide you from where you are to where you need or want to go.

Mastering change is a skill. Learn it, apply it, and practice it to achieve personal growth, development, and fulfillment.

By understanding how change affects global, national, societal, and personal levels, and by learning and applying strategies to respond thoughtfully and effectively, you can turn change into a tool for success—rather than letting it become a source of stress. Learning to anticipate, accept, and respond appropriately to your unique circumstances is vital for developing self-mastery.

Phase One is the first step in a three-phase program designed to help you understand and navigate your change with clarity, balance, and purpose. Here, we'll focus on mastering yourself—the essential skill for meaningful transformation.

Throughout the upcoming modules, you'll explore the crossroads of decision-making—when to address urgent needs, when to pursue deeper desires that align with your values, and when to seek stability. You'll learn to use self-awareness to identify your strengths and weaknesses. You'll also examine your beliefs and assumptions, learning to suspend judgment enough to see new possibilities and perspectives.

You'll gain clarity about what you can control, what you can influence, and how to release what's beyond your reach. You'll begin to develop a mindset that welcomes change and growth, and you'll examine how your values shape your sense of purpose.

From there, you'll discover practical ways to develop and demonstrate personal change strategies tailored to your unique situation. We'll end with a reminder about the importance of taking good care of yourself throughout your journey.

The modules include self-assessments and reflections designed to help you apply these insights to your own life, building confidence through self-mastery rather than blind optimism. Once you finish Phase One, you'll be prepared to approach personal change with balance—neither resisting nor over-pursuing it.

You'll then be ready to move on to *Phase Two: Shape Your Environment*, to support the person you're becoming. Having mastered yourself first, you'll realize that achieving change isn't about forcing it but about shaping what you can, given your unique situation, with intention, balance, and wisdom.

Then, in *Phase Three: Plan and Execute*, you'll learn how to develop and follow a clear plan of action with particular steps to achieve your goals and make lasting change.

Decision Point: To Change or Not?

Life is a journey filled with key moments that prompt us to pause and consider where we are and where we need or want to go.

Whether it's a once-in-a-lifetime opportunity, sudden job loss, health scare, or the result of introspection, we often find ourselves at a crossroads. Here, we face a vital choice: hold on to what's familiar or let go and seek change. This decision is more than a fleeting moment; it can shape our lifelong journey of wellbeing.

Throughout our lives, we'll encounter many crossroads, each requiring a decision on whether to change. These decisions often vary in form and urgency. An important point in this training is that, when contemplating change, *there is no one-size-fits-all solution*. Change requires a personalized approach, tailored to our individual circumstances and current stage of life.

The reasons that motivate us to change or keep us in the status quo are deeply personal. No matter where we are, we see our crossroads from three perspectives, each shaped by our internal needs and desires and external realities.

1. Choosing to Meet Our Needs

Life will bring challenges that require our attention, such as health issues, emotional difficulties, or unexpected financial difficulties.

During these critical moments, the *need* to change becomes a matter of survival. Small, intentional adjustments might be more effective than large, sweeping ones. By focusing on meeting our core needs, we regain stability.

Focusing on our needs improves our capacity to grow, develop, and achieve our long-term goals.

Crucially, we take the necessary actions to meet our needs, as unmet needs can cause stress that builds over time. Therefore, to manage stress effectively, we prioritize meeting our needs.

An overarching theme of this training program is addressing your stress. Plan accordingly.

2. Choosing to Pursue Our Wants

As our needs are met, we become better able to pursue our passions. This is where the shift from simply meeting needs to satisfying our *wants* happens. It offers an opportunity driven by curiosity and enthusiasm, where we actively seek experiences that enrich our lives.

However, we must be discerning; not every desire results in lasting change. A lifetime of growth should mirror our true selves and align with our values and vision for the future. On our journey, it's essential to avoid chasing fads or quick fixes, as these can distract us from real progress and often lead us back to where we started, facing the same unresolved issues.

3. Choosing Stability—for Now

At certain points in life, everything seems to be in harmony. Our careers, health, and relationships provide us with a sense of stability that doesn't require change. During these times, keeping the status quo is a sensible choice.

While we are satisfied with the current situation for now, it's important to understand that maintaining this state is not a permanent solution. We must remain aware of the changes occurring within us and around us. Acknowledging that change is inevitable—regardless of how comfortable we feel at the moment—will help us prepare to respond effectively when change becomes necessary or once again desired.

Being content today, while accepting that we'll face a crossroads again sooner or later, keeps us prepared for what's ahead.

The Overlap

These three perspectives—needing to change, wanting to change, and no need to change for now—often coexist.

For example, we might need to find a job quickly, want to pursue a new diet, while still valuing the stability of our relationships and routines. Real life isn't one-dimensional, and we must constantly adapt to our circumstances.

Recognizing these layers helps us prioritize in a healthy, psychologically balanced way. Needs come first, not because wants are unimportant, but because unmet needs drain the energy we rely on to pursue our desires. When we focus on what's essential, we strengthen the foundation that allows us to grow into what we want while maintaining what's already working well.

That's life's balancing act.

Understanding the type of change we face—whether it's pressure, desire, or stability—helps us respond thoughtfully. Each decision we make becomes an act of self-guidance, shaping not only our path but also who we are becoming. When we choose with clarity, we chart a journey that honors both our wellbeing and our aspirations.

Every decision matters; it shapes our journey and defines who we are. By making intentional choices at these crossroads, we carve our own path toward a more meaningful life.

So, When It's Time to Change, Change What?

A behavioral formula introduced by psychologist Kurt Lewin, regarded as the founder of modern social psychology, serves as a useful guide for our ongoing pursuit of self-improvement.

His formula is: B = f(P, E).

Lewin suggests that our behavior (B) is a function (f) of us (the person, P) and our environment (E), and that P and E are interdependent variables, meaning each influences and is influenced by the other.[1]

To achieve the change we need or want, we can alter our thinking (alter P), modify our environment (alter E), or change both (alter P and E). The formula suggests that changing our thoughts (P) can lead to new behaviors within the same environment. Similarly, changes in our environment (E) can influence our behavior. In this case, we might try to improve our current environment or leave it altogether as we pursue the change we need or want. Alternatively, we can modify both our thoughts and environment to reach our self-improvement goals.

Changing our thoughts and/or environment is essential for personal change, such as breaking bad habits and establishing and maintaining beneficial ones.

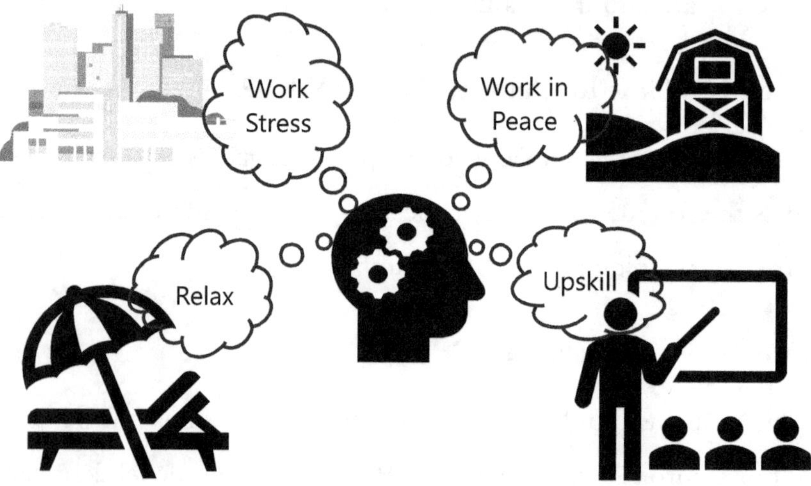

Figure I.1 Thinking About Four Scenarios

Referring to Figure I.1 above, the following four scenarios are based on Kurt Lewin's behavioral formula, $B = f(P, E)$, where behavior is a function of the person and their environment.

Scenario 1: Altering P Without Changing E

GC is a senior manager at a busy tech company in a major city. He enjoys his job, but long hours, a tiring subway commute, and constant deadline pressure lead to a cycle of stress—and, in particular, overeating.

Through self-awareness, GC realizes that the problem isn't just the environment—it's how he reacts to it. So instead of giving in to convenience foods at work, he makes a conscious change: he prepares all his meals at home and brings lunch with him every day.

This simple change in his daily routine—adopting mindful eating and cooking at home—led to a 30-pound weight loss over six months. Additionally, his physical strength grew, his focus sharpened, and his sleep became deeper. This straightforward dietary adjustment noticeably changed how he looks, thinks, and feels.

Best of all, it was sustainable, showing him that even in a high-stress work environment, a well-chosen personal tweak can significantly boost his wellbeing. This scenario illustrates Lewin's principle that, even though GC's environment (E) remains stressful, his intentional change in routine (alter P) allows him to succeed within it.

Scenario 2: Altering E Without Changing P

CS is a freelance graphic designer who moved to a big city in search of its promise of excitement, energy, and endless opportunities. Although her daily habits and routines are strong—she eats well, exercises, and tries to maintain a good work-life balance—her environment worked against her.

Constant street noise, a cramped apartment in disrepair, sky-high rent, and parking hassles continually drained her energy. Initially, trying city life seemed worthwhile. However, she realized that the mismatch between who she is—someone who thrives in calm, nature-filled spaces—and her living situation in a loud, crowded city caused stress and burnout.

After reflecting, CS decided to move back to a smaller town. The change didn't alter her as a person—her habits, routines, and work style remained the same, but it immediately boosted her wellbeing. By changing her environment, she regained her balance, calm, and focus.

This example highlights Lewin's insight that behavior and wellbeing are shaped by both personal traits and our surroundings. Often, the most effective way to promote change isn't just through self-discipline but by adjusting our environment to better support the life we want.

Scenario 3: Altering Both P and E

WJ worked as a customer service representative but began considering a career as a data analyst—a role that excited him and offered the potential for greater rewards. He recognized the gap between where he was and where he wanted to be. His skills and abilities (P) weren't enough to qualify him for his desired job, and his workplace (E) didn't provide the career growth opportunities he was looking for.

To improve his career, WJ took a two-pronged approach. He dedicated evenings and weekends to learning data analyst skills, steadily building competence and confidence (altering P). At the same time, he began looking for a new position at a different company that better aligned with his career goals (altering E). After six months of dedication—studying, sharpening his skills and abilities, networking, and applying to new companies—he landed a data analyst role at a firm known for its supportive culture and plenty of growth opportunities.

WJ's journey of self-improvement illustrates how newly acquired skills (P) and the external environment (E) influence one another. Lasting change often requires us to develop internally while also placing ourselves in an environment that promotes that growth.

Scenario 4: No Change Needed—for Now (P and E are in Harmony)

DS is a successful entrepreneur who has carefully built a career that offers her both financial security and personal freedom.

She has a strong support network, enjoys her work, and maintains a healthy work-life balance. Currently, her personal habits and routines (P) and her environment (E) are in harmony, and she is content.

Because her needs are met and her career goals are achieved, she doesn't feel pressured to make any changes. Instead, she chooses to enjoy the moment—taking a month-long vacation to rest and recharge.

This isn't an escape; it's a renewal.

DS's situation demonstrates homeostasis in real life: when our habits, routines, and environment are in harmony, we can pause our pursuit of change and enjoy the benefits of balance.

The following table summarizes these four scenarios.

Scenario	Example	Focus of Change	Outcome
1. Altering P (Person)	GC changes his eating habits (mindful eating and meal prep) while keeping the same environment.	Personal habits and self-regulation (P).	Weight loss, improved focus, sustained wellbeing despite unchanged work stressors.
2. Altering E (Environment)	CS relocates from a noisy, expensive city to a calmer small town, keeping the same healthy routines.	External environment and context (E).	Reduced stress and burnout, improved balance, calmer lifestyle.
3. Altering Both P and E	WJ gains new data skills (P) and moves to a new job with better growth (E).	Alter both skills (P) and environment (E).	Career transition, fulfillment, supportive work environment.
4. No Change Needed (P and E in Harmony)	DS already has strong habits and a balanced environment; she takes a vacation to recharge, no change required.	Neither P nor E require change; both are aligned.	Sustained balance, wellbeing, and renewal through rest.

Table I.1 Four Scenarios for P and E

In short, Lewin's formula tells us that behavior is not just "who we are" or "where we are"—it's the dynamic interaction between the two. Our actions emerge from the interplay between our traits, beliefs, habits, and readiness, and the cues, constraints, and pressures of our environment.

Of course, many of us can relate to this idea. For example, we probably have experienced a shift in our thoughts and actions if we have:

- Moved to a new, distant place, where we changed our habits, routines, attitudes, and preferences. This move might have been to attend college, where exposure to different perspectives and intellectual challenges broadened our worldview.

- Joined the military, where a highly structured and disciplined environment transformed our sense of responsibility, teamwork, and decision-making.

- Started a new job, and as a result, the workplace culture, leadership styles, and professional expectations influenced our work ethic and problem-solving methods.

- Either moved in with someone else or had someone move in with us, which changed our daily habits and routines.

- Got married, making a significant commitment that changed our responsibilities and expectations in relationships.

- Welcomed children into our lives, deeply transforming our perspectives, priorities, and daily routines.

- Experienced the loss of a loved one, suffered a serious physical injury, or endured a life-altering illness, which impacted our emotional wellbeing, coping mechanisms, and how we interact with our environment.

Mastering Ourselves

Phase One prepares you for change through self-mastery—the ability to intentionally steer your growth and your path. It's not about fixing everything all at once; it's about focusing on what you can control inside (P) and influence outside (E) to shape your life.

That means understanding the forces inside you—your beliefs, assumptions, values, habits, strengths and weaknesses, and personality (your P)—as well as the environments where you live, work, and connect with others (your E). By learning how to control P and influence E, you gain the ability to build a life that aligns with who you are and who you want to become.

Who you are right now, in this moment and place, is the focus of Phase One: identifying where internal change can support your growth. From there, it's about making deliberate choices, setting achievable goals, and shaping your environment: *Control P and influence E.*

Instead of waiting for circumstances to define you, self-mastery enables you to take action now—whether that's forming new habits, breaking old ones, developing skills, or cultivating resilience and perspective.

Ultimately, self-mastery involves continuously adjusting to our personal circumstances. It is the ability to face life's challenges with resilience, to align our actions with our goals and values, and to accomplish meaningful, lasting change on our own terms based on who and where we are.

What you'll learn here is rooted in decades of experience in initiating, leading, and sustaining change at different levels. I've used these tools not only to transform myself but also to help others and guide teams through lasting organizational change.

My goal is to share these lessons with you so you can use them today to make the change you need or want.

Takeaways

- There are three perspectives on change: (1) *needing* to change, (2) *wanting* to change, and (3) having *no reason* to change. The need for change can stem from high stress, and our focus is on addressing it. The self-assessment for this module offers insights that can help us in this effort.

- Lewin's fundamental equation B = f(P, E) indicates that our behavior (B) is a function (f) of both our personal traits (P) and our environment (E).

- In Phase One, we examine our thoughts (the P in the equation) and introduce timeless concepts, tools, and techniques to alter how we think. This helps us improve the internal conditions needed for meaningful change. In Phase Two, we focus on shaping external conditions (the E in the equation) to promote personal growth and development.

- There isn't a one-size-fits-all answer for self-improvement. What works for us is uniquely tailored to who we are and where we are in life, and it's up to us to discover, apply, and prove to ourselves what that is.

- Hope isn't a strategy. To achieve the change we need or want, we must take action.

- Nothing too much: Lasting personal change comes from balance—knowing ourselves and our environment, acting intentionally instead of excessively, and finding what uniquely works for us through purposeful effort.

When it comes to self-improvement, doing something is better than doing nothing. So, let's do something right now!

Stress Survey

Life happens, and it can cause both positive and negative stress that may build up over time. It's important to recognize and manage this stress.

The following survey is based on a revised version of the original Social Readjustment Rating Scale (SRRS), also known as the Holmes–Rahe Stress Inventory.[2] This adaptation draws from Wallace et al. (2023), published in PLOS ONE under the Creative Commons Attribution License (CC BY).[3]

Understanding Your Stress Level

In 1967, psychiatrists Thomas Holmes and Richard Rahe sought to answer a simple yet meaningful question: How do life changes affect our health?

Through extensive research, the researchers found that major life changes—whether positive or negative—require psychological adjustment, which can affect both mental and physical health.

They designed the Social Readjustment Rating Scale (SRRS), which lists 43 common life events linked to stress. Each event is assigned a Life Change Unit (LCU) score indicating the typical level of stress it can cause. For example, the death of a spouse carries the highest weight at 100 LCUs, with divorce ranking second at 73 LCUs, while less severe events like taking a vacation (13 LCUs) or receiving a traffic ticket (11 LCUs) have significantly lower scores.

Notably, positive life changes—such as getting married, starting a new job, or reaching a major milestone—can also increase your overall stress because your mind and body still need time to adjust.

Why This Matters

When many recent life changes add up—even small ones—your stress level can rise without you noticing. By becoming aware of your total "life change score," you'll better understand why you might feel drained, tense, or off balance—and which parts of your life may need more focus.

How to Use This Tool

- Review all 43 Life Events listed in the following table.
- Check off each event you've experienced in the last 12 months.
- Sum the Life Change Units (LCUs) for all checked events.
- Then, compare your total with the Stress Level Guide to evaluate your overall stress level.

Your score isn't about judgment; it's about self-awareness. It can help you decide where to slow down, prioritize actions, seek support, or make space for recovery.

Introduction

Social Readjustment Rating Scale (adapted from original source, 1967)
43 Life Events and Associated Life Change Units (LCUs)

Life Event	LCUs	☑	Life Event	LCUs	☑
1. Death of a spouse or life partner	100		23. Son or daughter leaving home	29	
2. Divorce	73		24. Trouble with in-laws	29	
3. Marital separation	65		25. Outstanding personal achievement	28	
4. Jail term	63		26. Spouse or life partner partner begins or stops work	26	
5. Death of close family member	63		27. Begin or end school	26	
6. Personal injury or illness	53		28. Change in living conditions	25	
7. Marriage	50		29. Revision of personal habits	24	
8. Losing your job	47		30. Trouble with boss	23	
9. Marital reconciliation	45		31. Change in work hours or conditions	20	
10. Retirement	45		32. Change in residence	20	
11. Change in health of family member	44		33. Change in schools	20	
12. Pregnancy (yourself or being the father)	40		34. Change in recreation	19	
13. Sex difficulties	39		35. Change in religious activities	19	
14. Gain of new family member	39		36. Change in social activities	18	
15. Business readjustment	39		37. Taking on a loan for a lesser purchase - e.g. car, college fees	17	
16. Change in financial state	38		38. Change in sleeping habits	16	
17. Death of close friend	37		39. Change in number of family get-togethers	15	
18. Change to different line of work	36		40. Change in eating habits	15	
19. Change in number of arguments with spouse or life partner	35		41. Vacation	13	
20. Taking on a mortgage or loan for a major purchase	31		42. Christmas	12	
21. Foreclosure of mortgage or loan	30		43. Minor violations of the law	11	
22. Change in responsibilities at work	29				

Table I.2 SRRS

Stress Level Guide

- 150 total points or fewer is considered relatively low risk.
- The 150–299 points range indicates moderate risk.
- 300 points or more indicate high risk.

Using a real-world example, we can demonstrate how Life Change Units accumulate and are measured on this scale.

18

Over 12 months, a couple gets married, which is #7 on the Life Events scale and equals 50 Life Change Units (LCUs).

Naturally, getting married then directly results in other life events, like a honeymoon, which is considered a vacation here and ranks #41 on the scale, adding 13 LCUs.

Then, getting pregnant (#12) adds 40 LCUs. Moving in together to a different, temporary rental unit (#32) adds 20 LCUs. Because that temporary change in residence is necessary for attendance at a school (#27), we add 26 LCUs.

After graduation, the family moves to a newly purchased house (#20), adding 31 LCUs. During these transitions, to stay at home full-time with the soon-to-be newborn, one spouse stops working (#26), adding 26 LCUs.

And with getting married, going on a honeymoon, getting pregnant, moving to a temporary rental unit to attend school, moving again after graduation into a newly purchased home, with one spouse transitioning out of the job market to stay home with the baby on the way, there's a significant change in social activities (#36), which adds 18 LCUs.

In summary, to outline how stress builds up from these life events over 12 months:

Life Event (Chronological Order)	LCUs
Marriage	50
Honeymoon	13
Pregnancy	40
1st Change in Residence	20
Attend School	26
Move to 2nd Residence, Buy Home	31
One Spouse Leaves Job Market to Stay Home with Newborn	26
Change in Social Activities	18
Total Holmes-Rahe Score	**224**

Table I.3 Sample of LCUs in One Year

A total score of 224 falls within the 150–299 range, indicating a moderate-to-elevated risk of stress-related health problems. This is typically described as roughly a 50% increase in the risk of developing a serious health issue within the next two years compared with scores below 150.

The scale is a rough predictive tool—it indicates increased overall life change but is not a diagnosis. It serves as a reminder to prioritize stress management and, if concerns are severe, to seek professional help.

In the Army, Soldiers and their families often experience significant stress due to frequent relocations to remote areas, attendance at various schools, and frequent job changes. This ongoing cycle of change can be overwhelming. To help manage the stress of this transient lifestyle, we receive training and guidance on recognizing and managing it. This support is provided through formal, mandatory programs such as "reception and integration," "in-processing" upon arrival for a new assignment, and "out-processing" before moving to the next location or transitioning out of the Army.

Of course, these experiences aren't unique to military life. Over time, each of us faces major life events—such as moving away for school, changing jobs, getting married, having children, buying a home, losing loved ones, or dealing with serious financial challenges—that bring their own stress levels.

Critically, stress can accumulate for all of us, even from positive events, since one life change can trigger a series of other changes. The Holmes-Rahe stress inventory provides a practical, self-assessment method for measuring these pressures, giving a rough estimate of the amount of change we're experiencing at any moment.

By making the invisible burden of stress visible and measurable, we can prioritize issues and plan to address that stress effectively.

This tool reminds us that life events happen and empowers us to respond with awareness, managing change and stress as they occur, while staying true to our values and long-term goals.

Next Up

Thinking about what you're thinking, with self-compassion.

Module 1: Practice Self-Awareness

Look within. Within is the fountain of good, and it will ever bubble up, if thou wilt ever dig.— Marcus Aurelius[4]

Learning Objectives. By the end of this module, you will be able to:

1. Practice self-reflection to examine your thoughts and actions, deepen understanding, boost resilience, and lessen harsh self-criticism.
2. Establish and maintain new habits and routines that encourage personal growth, while evaluating boundaries that help prevent overthinking and sustain balance.
3. Assess and leverage your strengths while improving weaknesses to enable opportunities for growth, aligning your self-improvement journey with your goals and aspirations.

What Is It?

Self-awareness lets us observe and reflect on our thoughts, choices, and actions with curiosity rather than judgment. This ability helps us spot patterns and triggers in our daily lives, giving us clarity to respond more thoughtfully rather than react automatically.

A deeper understanding of ourselves also involves exploring the underlying factors that shape who we are, including our beliefs, assumptions, values, habits, aptitudes, and personality traits. By examining these influences, we gain insight into how they shape our choices and interactions.

This kind of reflection connects our actions more directly to our true selves, promoting intentional growth and change. Most importantly, self-awareness isn't about harsh self-criticism but about developing a compassionate and objective perspective. When we approach our inner world with openness, we foster greater empathy for ourselves and, in turn, for others.

Over time, this continual pursuit of self-discovery cultivates deeper connections, a stronger sense of purpose, and a more engaged life.

Why It Matters

Our thoughts shape how we respond to the world. They influence the choices we make, the habits we develop, and ultimately the path our lives take. If we want to change our behavior or grow in meaningful ways, we first need to learn how to notice our thoughts—not to judge them, but to understand them more clearly.

This is where self-awareness becomes crucial. It serves as the foundation for other self-management skills, including self-reflection: the ability to look back on your experiences and recognize what has influenced your reactions, patterns, and beliefs. Without that awareness, change often stays reactive or short-term.

As you begin to recognize the patterns that impact your responses, you gain more options. You can start aligning your actions with what matters most to you instead of operating on autopilot. Over time, this kind of awareness naturally prompts deeper questions—not just as abstract ideas, but as lived questions: Who am I becoming? What do I want my life to represent?

Through self-awareness, we can:

- Identify and focus on key areas for growth. This broad, general approach to self-improvement underscores the importance of understanding our strengths and weaknesses.

- Identify stress triggers. By recognizing our triggers and managing stress, we can reduce or eliminate it through changes to our habits and routines.

- Make better-informed decisions that reflect our core values. This highlights the importance of a decision-making process that aligns our choices with our authentic selves.

- Set realistic goals. This emphasizes the importance of establishing meaningful, achievable, and sustainable goals that meet our needs and fulfill our wants, while considering our strengths, weaknesses, and values.

- Build greater confidence in reaching those goals. This emphasizes the importance of strengthening our self-assurance in achieving what we need and want. The more we succeed, the more we can accomplish in the future.

Practical Application

Self-awareness deepens our understanding of our thoughts, emotions, and behavior patterns, making lasting change more attainable. By examining the beliefs, assumptions, values, habits, and traits that influence our actions, we establish the conditions necessary for intentional change.

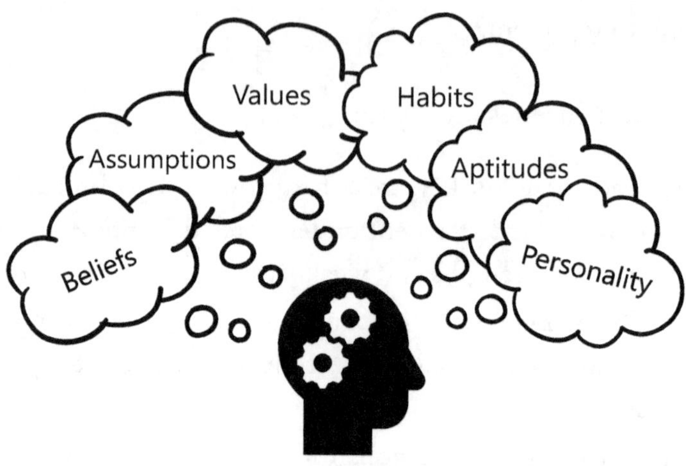

Figure 1.1 Being Self-Aware

For example, if we think we're not good at public speaking and tend to avoid it, we can examine why we feel this way without judgment or harsh self-criticism. This reflection helps us see public speaking as a valuable, career-enhancing skill to develop rather than something to fear and avoid.

Gaining confidence in public speaking involves stepping outside our comfort zones. While we may feel comfortable talking with friends and close associates, taking a small step to speak in a larger, unfamiliar setting can help us gain valuable experience and boost confidence. This might include sharing our thoughts more broadly than usual, such as in a workplace meeting or classroom, where we believe we have useful insights to offer.

Self-improvement revolves around making meaningful changes. Awareness of our thoughts—paying attention to what we're thinking, feeling, and how that affects our actions—is essential. By understanding why we think and act as we do, and pinpointing what we need or want to change, we can shift our thinking to encourage new behaviors. In public speaking, this awareness could lead to forming a new habit that offers significant benefits.

In summary, self-awareness enables us to change our thinking, which in turn influences our actions. We can begin shifting our thinking today by practicing introspection and self-evaluation.

Introspection is a reflective process that encourages us to consider our thoughts, choices, and actions with compassion. Given our current situation, it's essential to identify what we need or want to improve and understand the reasons behind those changes. When we clarify our needs, wants, and values, we can design a positive growth plan that aligns with who we aim to become.

Self-evaluation enhances awareness by analyzing how our behaviors and habits support or impede our goals. Also, recognizing our strengths allows us to use them effectively, while identifying our weaknesses highlights areas for growth. With this understanding, we can focus on what matters most and take intentional steps toward meaningful change.

Challenges and Pitfalls

Self-awareness promotes personal growth by enhancing our understanding of ourselves. However, this skill also brings challenges and risks.

When introspection becomes too intense, it can easily turn into rumination—an unproductive cycle where we repeatedly replay past mistakes and dwell on negative experiences. This can leave us feeling stuck, caught in a loop that keeps us from moving forward.

To achieve balance, it's important to develop a habit of compassionate inward reflection. Reflecting on our thoughts and feelings doesn't have to involve harsh self-criticism. Instead, we can examine ourselves with curiosity and seek to understand our motivations and emotions without criticizing our flaws. This positive approach to reflection makes self-awareness a powerful tool rather than a trap.

Marcus Aurelius's insight is especially relevant here. His advice to "look within" encourages us to access the inner strength that resides within each of us. According to Aurelius, this source of strength is unlimited if we keep exploring it with an open mind.

Through self-reflection, we gain valuable insights that support our personal growth. We learn to identify our strengths and accept our flaws, paving a clearer path to self-improvement.

This inner journey helps us recognize areas for growth and reminds us of the resilience and potential we already have. We aim to make reflection a helpful habit. With the right balance, self-awareness can reveal who we are. We can identify our strengths while also pinpointing areas for improvement, all without falling into the trap of self-criticism.

When we practice reflection, we enhance our self-awareness and tap into the endless reserve of strength within us, fostering growth and healing along the way.

Timeless Wisdom

Developing self-awareness—spending time to reflect on our thoughts—is a timeless sign of wisdom.

For thousands of years, leaders and philosophers have shared a common truth: greatness starts from within. As he guided the Roman Empire, Marcus Aurelius reminded himself daily to "look within." The ancient Greeks engraved "Know thyself" into stone. Chinese thinkers advocated harmony through self-understanding by "looking inward." These voices from the past echo through history with one consistent message: self-awareness is the foundation for growth.

That timeless insight is not limited to history books—for example, it remains relevant today through the guiding U.S. Army leadership principle: "Know yourself and seek self-improvement."[5] This principle encourages us to be brutally honest about our strengths and weaknesses, not as a form of judgment but as a plan for growth. Recognizing our strengths allows us to lead with confidence, inspire others, and face challenges boldly. Admitting our weaknesses opens the door to growth, resilience, and transformation.

A classic example can be seen in ancient Greece, where a dialogue with the philosopher Socrates (470-399 BCE) is presented in Plato's *Charmides*.

In *Charmides*, Plato records Socrates' conversation with Critias about the Delphic maxim "Know Thyself," one of three inscriptions at the Temple of Apollo.[6]

Critias interprets the phrase as a call for temperance, suggesting that the god urged people to greet one another not with the usual "Hail!" but with a reminder to practice moderation and self-control.

Socrates emphasizes this point even more. For him, self-knowledge isn't just about restraint but about wisdom itself: the ability to recognize what you know and, more importantly, what you don't. He argues that humility in the face of ignorance is the start of wisdom.

The dialogue highlights a timeless truth: growth relies on self-awareness. To "know thyself" means honestly reflecting on one's abilities, limits, and blind spots. It's about balancing ambition with reality and encouraging moderation and curiosity, and this Delphic wisdom remains as relevant today as it was in Socrates' Athens.

Before Socrates, we refer to the ancient Chinese philosopher Confucius, who lived from 551 to 479 BCE. On looking inward, he taught:[7]

> When we see men of worth, we should think of equaling them; when we see men of a contrary character, we should turn inwards and examine ourselves.

Here, Confucius teaches that encounters with others should prompt us to examine ourselves. This wisdom reminds us that every interaction is an opportunity to grow. When we meet people of integrity, insight, or courage, we should aim to emulate and embody these virtues. Similarly, when we notice negative qualities in others, the first step isn't to criticize but to reflect on whether we share those flaws.

In this way, both the admirable and the unpleasant serve as mirrors. Each reflection helps us see more clearly who we are, where we fall short, and how we might grow. For Confucius, self-awareness is not abstract—it's a daily discipline, shaped by the examples around us and guided by the humility to look inward before casting judgment outward.

Finally, we turn to the wisdom of the *Tao Te Ching*, also translated as *The Classic of the Way and Its Power*. This book is traditionally credited to Lao Tzu, who is believed to have lived in China during the 6th century BCE and to have served as a high-ranking official in the Chinese Empire.

According to legend, Lao Tzu was dissatisfied with the government's charade and left the country, riding on a water buffalo. As he was leaving China, an impressed border guard asked him to write down his thoughts, which he did before departing. After that, he was never seen again. Regarding mastering ourselves, Lao Tzu said:[8]

> He who knows other men is discerning;
> he who knows himself is intelligent.
>
> He who overcomes others is strong;
> he who overcomes himself is mighty.
>
> He who is satisfied with his lot is rich;
> he who goes on acting with energy has a firm
> will.

In this passage, Lao Tzu highlights that wisdom comes from self-awareness—understanding our thoughts, actions, strengths, and weaknesses. Being self-aware enhances our intelligence, guiding us through life with clarity.

True power comes from mastering ourselves rather than dominating others. Self-control, informed by awareness, helps us overcome internal struggles that hinder our personal growth. It emphasizes developing inner strength rather than chasing external victories. Self-awareness encourages contentment by helping us understand our needs, desires, and limits, leading to satisfaction as we progress. Conscious actions, grounded in our awareness, support aligned ambition instead of aimless pursuits.

In short, Lao Tzu suggests that true intelligence, strength, and contentment come from understanding and mastering ourselves, ultimately leading to personal fulfillment and a balanced life.

Taken together, these lasting voices convey a clear lesson: greatness starts from within.

In everyday life, this wisdom encourages us to pause, observe, and reflect. Every decision, interaction, and challenge offers a chance to ask: What can I learn about myself in this moment?

Understanding ourselves means taking responsibility for who we are and who we are becoming. It also involves aligning our actions with our values, transforming weaknesses into strengths, and directing our energy toward meaningful growth.

From timeless wisdom, we learn that when we control ourselves, we unlock the ability to grow, lead, and become our best selves.

Anecdote: Making It a Habit

It's one of those things in life that many of us fear. Speaking to an audience with all eyes and ears on us can be a humbling, nerve-wracking, or even anxiety-inducing experience.

Although public speaking can make us so uncomfortable that we avoid it altogether, it plays a vital role in our personal and professional development. It's essential for various pursuits, especially when advancing one's career in many fields.

For example, as we advance in our careers, we may become "the face of the organization." This means that at some point, we might be expected to participate in and lead meetings, brief senior managers and leaders, join question-and-answer sessions on our expertise, and deliver presentations to influence people beyond our immediate colleagues.

If we're aiming for a position that probably requires public speaking, how can we develop the skill to be good, or at least good enough, at it?

We do it.

Through self-awareness, we identify our strengths—including our expertise, which qualifies us for our current role or next promotion—and our weaknesses, such as a lack of confidence in public speaking and a tendency to avoid it altogether.

Without judgment, we recognize our tendency to avoid public speaking and work to build the habit. That is, we shift our perspective from viewing public speaking as something to avoid to recognizing its benefits.

Once again, we turn to timeless wisdom to better guide our journey of self-improvement.

In *Nicomachean Ethics,* Aristotle (384 - 322 BCE) outlined the concept of virtue ethics, in which virtues are cultivated through habit. He said:[9]

> For the things we have to learn before we can do them, we learn by doing them, e.g. men become builders by building and lyre-players by playing the lyre; so too we become just by doing just acts, temperate by doing temperate acts, brave by doing brave acts.

Aristotle emphasizes that our self-development requires action and practice. We do it to become skilled at it. Personal growth and experience are not achieved through passive learning but through consistent, practical application.

In summarizing Aristotle's idea of habituation, author Will Durant famously said:[10]

> Excellence is an art won by training and
> habituation: we do not act rightly because we
> have virtue or excellence, but we rather have
> these because we have acted rightly.
>
> We are what we repeatedly do. Excellence, then,
> is not an act but a habit.

Self-improvement comes from consistent effort and habits, not isolated actions. We prioritize developing positive, productive routines over time rather than depending on occasional bursts of intense, unsustainable effort.

Although change is often easier said than done, the main point is that we need to take action, not just think about it.

And action involves stepping outside our comfort zone to transform a perceived weakness into a strength.

Know Yourself and Seek Self-Improvement

It's an Army principle that stays with you for life.

Many of us tend to shy away from what we fear. For me, that fear was public speaking. But in the Army, avoiding it wasn't an option—my career depended on it.

In the Army's up-or-out promotion system, there was no confusion about the requirement: if I didn't advance to a certain rank by a specific time, I would definitely be discharged. It was that simple.

Getting promoted involved facing intimidating senior noncommissioned officers (NCOs) at promotion boards, speaking clearly and confidently while answering all their questions, and earning their recommendation for promotion.

The problem? I had never been part of a public question-and-answer session before, and the thought of it made my chest tighten. My gut told me to avoid it, but self-awareness pushed me to be honest: if I didn't face this fear, my career could be over.

To stay in, I had to earn promotions on time, which meant passing two consecutive promotion boards.

To overcome my weakness, I chose a challenging yet realistic way to prepare for the promotion board—I entered a Soldier of the Month competition.

When I entered the boardroom, my Class A uniform looked sharp, and my posture was steady, but my palms were sweating. Facing a panel of senior NCOs, I felt my heart pounding so loudly I was sure they could hear it.

Then came the first question. I answered it. Then another. And another. By the end, I hadn't just survived the ordeal—I had won the competition!

This one event changed everything.

If I hadn't taken that initial, monumental, nerve-wracking step and faced the board, my Army service would have ended after just a few years, and my entire life's trajectory would have been much different.

My first board appearance proved I could accomplish what once seemed impossible. From that point on, I made it a routine to study, prepare, and step into situations that challenged me. Throughout my active-duty career, I appeared before seven competition and promotion boards, each of which helped build my confidence as public speaking shifted from my greatest fear to one of my greatest strengths.

It all began with knowing myself and seeking self-improvement—having the courage to admit a weakness, and the willingness to face discomfort to turn it into a strength.

And that's the lesson: when you're honest about where you need to grow and bold enough to take action to improve yourself, you turn weakness into strength.

Takeaways

- Being self-aware is essential for planned personal change.
- Self-awareness remains free from judgment and harsh criticism.
- We leverage our strengths, address our weaknesses, and stay focused on our goals.
- Developing new habits is one way to achieve and maintain meaningful change.
- The idea of understanding ourselves better to improve ourselves is as old as human history—and as relevant today as ever.

- Nothing too much: Self-awareness is vital for personal growth, but overthinking can cause anxiety.

End of Module 1 – Deepening Self-Awareness

Whether you're focusing on personal growth or planning your next moves in school, training, or your career, gathering clear information about your strengths, weaknesses, and tendencies can be especially helpful.

Aptitude tests, academic assessments, skills matchers, and personality self-assessments each provide a different perspective on how you tend to think, learn, and interact with the world. No single tool reveals the complete picture—and some are more dependable than others—but together, they can help you make better, more realistic decisions.

Used effectively, these tools supplement personal reflection, feedback from others, and real-world experience rather than substituting them.

By early adulthood, most people exhibit relatively stable patterns in broad abilities (such as cognitive strengths and learning styles) and personality traits—how we generally think, feel, relate, and respond to challenges. These patterns are not fixed or destiny-shaping, but they are fairly consistent. They tend to recur across jobs, relationships, and life stages, even as circumstances change.

When these patterns are ignored, people often set expectations that don't match how they operate, leading to frustration, burnout, or repeated mistakes. Recognizing them doesn't limit growth—it offers a practical starting point. Self-awareness helps you work with your tendencies instead of against them, making change more deliberate and sustainable.

Millions of people in the U.S. take aptitude, academic, and skills tests each year and often gain a clearer understanding of where they feel confident and where they might need support or growth. For self-improvement, the value isn't in the score itself—it's in what you learn about how you approach problems, respond to pressure, stay focused, and engage with unfamiliar tasks.

If you haven't already—or if it's been a while—it's always a good idea to learn more about yourself. Whether you're in your teens, twenties, thirties, or older, you can start small and risk-free. A short practice test can serve as a baseline. A prep book can reveal patterns in how you think. A full-length test can show how you handle time limits, complexity, and sustained effort.

These experiences can be humbling—and enlightening. They aren't meant to label or confine you. They offer clues. You interpret what those clues mean and how to use them. The goal isn't perfection or comparison—it's awareness. And with increased awareness, you make better choices, build more confidence, and find a clearer path forward.

It's never too early or too late to gain a clearer understanding of yourself.

Note: The resources mentioned here are publicly available practice tests and self-assessments meant for skill exploration. They are not official testing events and do not lead to recruitment, admissions, or score reporting.

Aptitude, Academic, and Skills

Five Tools for Building Self-Awareness and Planning Your Growth

Long before we take an exam for the military, college, or a new job, we have already been evaluated in many ways. In school, we were assessed through quizzes, reading and math benchmarks, science labs, group projects, fitness tests, report cards, and direct teacher feedback.

These early experiences provided insights into how we think and learn—what comes naturally, what takes extra effort, and how we approach challenges, structure, or hands-on activities. This kind of feedback is especially valuable because it shows that self-awareness isn't just about inward reflection; it's about recognizing patterns in your abilities, strengths, and habits.

That same pattern-spotting continues later in life through standardized tests and skills assessments that reveal how we process information and approach challenges.

In the U.S., standardized tests like the ASVAB, SAT, and ACT are often linked to young adults. However, their purpose—gaining insights into how people process information, solve problems, and apply knowledge—is useful at any age.

If you're seeking age-neutral options, tools such as the CareerOneStop Skills Matcher and MyNextMove.org provide helpful insights without needing a formal testing setup. Unlike the ASVAB, SAT, and ACT, these tools rely on self-reported interests and preferences to suggest careers.

Here's an overview of five tools you can explore based on your goals and interests.

ASVAB – Armed Services Vocational Aptitude Battery

- **What it assesses:** Knowledge and skills in math, science, word comprehension, mechanical understanding, and related technical areas. Over one million people take it each year.[11]
- **How it helps:** Although primarily used for military specialty placement, the ASVAB also highlights strengths in analytical, mechanical, and problem-solving skills that are applicable to many careers. These insights can help you pursue skilled trades, technical training, or entrepreneurial opportunities where hands-on and logical abilities are important.
- **Free prep:** Army-sponsored test practice and diagnostics are available at March2Success.com.[12]

SAT

- **What it assesses:** Reading, writing, and math skills designed to predict readiness for college-level work. According to the College Board, more than two million students in the high school class of 2025 took the SAT.[13]
- **How it helps:** A free practice SAT isn't just for college-bound students; it's a low-pressure way to see how well you handle

real-world skills like reading complex information, interpreting data, and making decisions under time constraints. Your results can reveal strengths to use and areas to improve, whether you're working on communication, preparing for training, or simply exploring your next step.

- **Free prep:** Khan Academy's Official SAT Practice offers adaptive, no-cost skill diagnostics.[14]

ACT

- **What it assesses:** English, math, reading, and science reasoning, plus an optional writing section. ACT reports 1.4 million U.S. high school graduates took its test in 2024.[15]

- **How it helps:** The ACT tests practical reasoning in English, math, reading, and science—giving a clear picture of how you interpret information, communicate ideas, and solve problems under time pressure. For adults, the free practice ACT, like the SAT, offers a low-stress way to see how you handle data, grasp complex material, and balance speed with accuracy, even if college isn't the immediate goal.

- **Free prep:** ACT.org offers free sample questions and full-length practice tests.[16]

CareerOneStop Skills Matcher (Sponsored by the U.S. Department of Labor)

- **What it assesses:** Your present skills versus the skills needed in hundreds of jobs.

- **How it helps:** This self-reporting tool is great for spotting transferable skills—strengths you already have that can be useful in a new field. It helps you identify training gaps, consider career changes, or determine which jobs match the skills you offer.

- **Free tools are available on their site.**[17]

MyNextMove.org (Sponsored by the U.S. Department of Labor and developed by the National Center for O*NET Development)

- **What it assesses:** Your interests and skills, then connects them to detailed job information, salary ranges, and education requirements.

- **How it helps:** MyNextMove turns self-discovery into practical career planning. It can guide you toward technical programs, help you plan community college coursework, or clarify what specific entrepreneurial paths entail.

- **Free tools are available on their site.**[18]

Using Tools for Self-Awareness—Not Self-Judgment

The value of tests like these lies in their structured way of highlighting potential strengths and areas for development—rather than in providing definitive answers. Similar self-knowledge can come from other sources, such as formal evaluations, workplace feedback, ongoing reflection, or lived experience.

The goal is not to depend on any single tool, but to increase your self-awareness as you work on change. Think of these assessments as mirrors rather than judgments—sources of insight, not judgments on intelligence or potential.

Used thoughtfully, they can help you recognize how you respond to challenges, where you tend to feel confident or uncertain, and what patterns influence your decisions. From that awareness, deliberate improvement becomes possible. As you explore, ask yourself:

- How did I handle frustration or uncertainty?
- Which tasks felt natural, and which required more effort?
- What thinking patterns kept recurring?
- How effectively did I manage my focus, time, and energy?
- What do these results indicate about my potential for growth?

Self-awareness deepens when you can honestly observe yourself—and intentionally use that insight. The clearer you understand your strengths and weaknesses, the better you can shape the future you want, without relying on guesswork.

Personality

Three Tools for Learning More About Our Tendencies

Our personality quietly influences almost everything we do—how we see the world, what we focus on, how we react under stress, and even the goals we're attracted to. These patterns appear in our preferences, habits, and reactions long before we become aware of them.

Becoming self-aware involves noticing these tendencies, not to label ourselves, but to understand the default settings that influence our choices. When we identify consistent patterns in how we think, feel, and act, we can choose our responses rather than operate on autopilot.

This clarity—honest and free of judgment—helps us use our natural strengths more effectively, avoid common pitfalls, and implement deliberate changes rather than rely on guesswork. Personality isn't a fixed identity; it's a set of tendencies. The more aware we are of them, the more freedom we have to grow.

Three tools that offer perspectives on personality are the Big Five (OCEAN), the Myers-Briggs Type Indicator (MBTI), and the Holland Code/RIASEC career-interest framework. These models vary in the extent of scientific evidence supporting them, but each offers practical language for understanding how you naturally perceive the world. The goal isn't to score yourself or fit into a category, but to gain insights you can use to guide your tendencies toward healthier, more meaningful outcomes.

A Sample of Three Personality Self-Assessments

1. Big Five (Five Factor) Model / OCEAN

The Big Five describes personality in terms of five broad, research-backed traits: Openness to Experience, Conscientiousness, Extraversion, Agreeableness, and Neuroticism (OCEAN). Unlike "type" systems that categorize you, the Big Five sees personality as a set of continuous scales—you're simply higher or lower on each trait.

Decades of peer-reviewed research demonstrate that these traits significantly predict real-life outcomes, including work habits, relationship patterns, emotional tendencies, and long-term wellbeing. That's why the Big Five remains one of the most respected and widely used personality frameworks in modern psychology.

One reliable, quick, and free Big Five test is provided by the Open-Source Psychometrics Project, consisting of 50 items that most people complete in about 3–8 minutes.[19]

This self-assessment provides a clear, trait-based snapshot of your personality. For example, you might find that you're high in conscientiousness but moderate in extraversion—insights you can use to better understand your motivations, improve decision-making, and recognize patterns that influence your daily life.

2. Myers-Briggs Type Indicator (MBTI) / MBTI-style assessments

This is one of the most popular frameworks that assesses preferences across four dichotomies: Extraversion versus Introversion; Sensing versus Intuition; Thinking versus Feeling; and Judging versus Perceiving. It then assigns one of 16 personality "types."

The Myers-Briggs company offers a free online version that provides your four-letter personality type.[20]

This model can assist by providing a recognizable type (such as ISFJ, ESFJ, or INTJ) that often resonates and offers a narrative about how you prefer to process information or make decisions. Importantly, use it as an insight tool rather than a fixed identity.

3. Holland Code (RIASEC) Model

This model links personality interest patterns to work and career settings, focusing on individuals rather than on general psychological traits. Developed by American Psychologist John L. Holland, it identifies six categories: Realistic, Investigative, Artistic, Social, Enterprising, and Conventional (RIASEC). The main idea is that people tend to be more satisfied and successful when their work environment matches their personality type.

In his 1973 book, *Making Vocational Choices: A Theory of Careers*, Holland included a self-assessment called "The Self-directed Search" (SDS).[21]

The model links your preferences and desired work environment with how your personality influences those choices. It connects "who you are" to "where you thrive."

Free online versions of the Holland Code assessments are available, including the O*Net Interest Profiler sponsored by the U.S. Department of Labor, which aligns with Holland's structure.[22]

Nothing Too Much: Use these tools to understand your consistent patterns in thinking, feeling, acting, and working, rather than to rigidly label yourself. Remember that your scores or types reflect tendencies, not fixed outcomes, and you can adapt, grow, and change over time. Treat your results as a starting point for more deliberate decisions, rather than as unchangeable categories.

SWOT Analysis

In the two earlier end-of-module sections, we saw how baseline aptitude, academic achievement, and personality self-assessments help us understand our thoughts and reasons for our actions. Together, they build on self-awareness—highlighting the natural talents we rely on and the tendencies that influence our decisions.[23]

This insight isn't about judgment; it's about clarity. When we recognize our strengths, weaknesses, and personal patterns, we can see more clearly where we excel and where we might need growth.

To deepen that awareness, the next step is to conduct an analysis using a straightforward yet effective framework called SWOT, which stands for Strengths, Weaknesses, Opportunities, and Threats. Although SWOT was originally designed for organizational planning, it can also be highly useful for personal growth.

Your self-awareness in these four areas can guide your planning. A personal SWOT analysis does more than just describe your situation; it helps you make smarter decisions, anticipate challenges, and pursue change with confidence and purpose. It's a tool for leveraging strengths, improving weaknesses, capitalizing on opportunities, and managing threats.

SWOT Analysis for Organizational Awareness

The SWOT analysis is a structured tool organizations use to assess their readiness for change across four key areas:

- **Strengths.** These are internal advantages within the organization that can support the proposed change, such as a skilled workforce and a strong reputation.
- **Weaknesses.** These internal limitations may impede change, such as resource shortages and inefficiencies.

- **Opportunities.** These are external factors (outside the organization) that can prompt change, such as emerging markets and new technologies.
- **Threats.** These external challenges, such as competition and economic shifts, could threaten the success of the change.

By identifying and visualizing these elements, leaders gain a clearer understanding of the organization's position, allowing them to craft strategies accordingly.

Applying SWOT Analysis to Managing Planned Personal Change

This same framework can be a useful tool for evaluating personal readiness when working toward a specific, prioritized change:

- **Strengths**. Regarding the specific change you need or want to make, consider your talents, skills, and personal qualities that enhance your confidence and resilience. Using your existing strengths helps you approach this change with clarity and momentum.
- **Weaknesses.** Identify habits, blind spots, skill gaps, or limitations that may hinder you. Recognizing these allows you to design realistic improvement plans and work toward achieving your change.
- **Opportunities:** Identify external resources, mentors, networks, or life circumstances to support your specific change.
- **Threats.** Identify external challenges such as time constraints, financial stress, or an unsupportive environment that could hinder your progress.

A SWOT analysis can turn vague self-reflections into a clear plan for personal growth and improvement. It promotes honesty about who we are and where we stand, strategic planning for where we want to go, and intentional management of the change journey.

SWOT Template for Personal Change

Strengths	**Weaknesses**
• What are my skills and talents regarding this particular change? • What personal qualities set me apart in terms of what I'm pursuing?	• Given what I want to change, what habits or lack of skills hold me back? • Where am I lacking confidence or consistency to make this change?
Opportunities	**Threats**
• What resources, mentors, or networks can I use for this change? • In terms of what I want to change, what new trends can I take advantage of?	• What external challenges could block the change I'm pursuing? • What risks or obstacles do I need to prepare for to achieve this change?

Figure 1.2 SWOT Analysis

The following is an example application of a SWOT analysis for a job change.

Referring to the Introduction, Scenario 3: Altering Both P and E, the following example demonstrates a SWOT Analysis for WJ as he considered a career transition to a Data Analyst role.

WJ's Strengths (Internal, Positive, Leverage)

- Displays a strong aptitude for office-based, white-collar work.
- Demonstrates skill with computer technology and adapts to new tools.
- Has previously shown persistence and discipline in upskilling to secure his current job.
- Possesses a proactive mindset in taking ownership of his career growth.

Weaknesses (Internal, Challenges, Improve)

- Although he wants a new role, he admits he lacks formal data analysis training, hands-on skills, and relevant experience.
- He'll need to more effectively manage his time and energy between his current full-time job, after-work activities, and the demanding training required to land the job he's aiming for.

Opportunities (External, Positive, Capitalize)

- Online resources, high-quality training platforms, and certification programs make upskilling accessible.
- There is a strong demand for data analyst positions in the local job market.
- Many tech companies in the region offer solid career opportunities and chances for advancement.
- There are networking opportunities available within the tech community.

Threats (External, Challenges, Manage)

- Being new to the field, there's a risk of rejection or delays in entering it.

- These are good jobs, but there's stiff competition from candidates with more data analyst training and experience, so his starting pay might reflect this reality.

- Rapidly advancing technology may require ongoing learning to stay competitive, and he'll need to plan accordingly.

Results: After six months of upskilling and networking, WJ successfully managed his transition by adjusting both his personal skills (altered P) and environment (altered E). By learning and becoming proficient with his new data analysis skills, he turned a weakness into a strength. By finding and joining a new company in a growing industry, he positioned himself in an environment that aligns with his long-term goals. His success demonstrates how personal growth and environmental fit mutually support career advancement.

Example: Using SWOT to Support Dietary Change—*Dual Goals: Weight Loss and Increased Energy*

A personal SWOT analysis helps you go beyond just relying on willpower and start crafting a plan that fits your real life. By identifying your internal strengths and weaknesses, along with the external opportunities and threats around you, you can make changes that feel more manageable, sustainable, and supportive.

Below is an example of how a SWOT analysis could be conducted for someone pursuing dietary change with the goals of weight loss and increased daily energy.

Strengths (Internal—Leverage)

Strengths are the personal qualities, habits, and resources you already have that can support change:

- Strong motivation to improve health and overall wellbeing.
- A strong understanding of fundamental nutrition.
- Genuine enjoyment of healthy foods makes change feel less restrictive.
- Generally skilled at planning, tracking, or organizing routines.

Leverage strengths, so you don't have to start from scratch.

Weaknesses (Internal—Improve)

Weaknesses aren't personal flaws; they are recurring patterns or limitations that need careful planning:

- Late-night snacking or emotional eating during stressful times.
- Feeling low on energy after work, which makes meal prep seem overwhelming.
- Doubt about consistency due to prior attempts at dietary change.
- Struggling to set boundaries around time, meals, or cravings.

Recognizing these patterns allows you to focus on improving them rather than resisting them.

Opportunities (External—Capitalize)

Opportunities are external elements in your environment that can help you achieve your goals:

- Access to affordable, healthy groceries, farmers' markets, or online grocery delivery.
- Supportive friends, family members, or coworkers who promote healthier choices.
- Local walking trails, gyms, or community wellness programs.
- Free apps and online tools for meal planning, tracking, and motivation.

These are resources you can deliberately use to make change easier.

Threats (External—Manage)

Threats are external pressures or conditions that raise the chance of setbacks:

- Busy, unpredictable, or lengthy work schedules.
- Frequent social gatherings centered around food.
- High-stress environments and fatigue.
- Home or workplace environments with convenient access to tempting foods.

Threats don't have to be eradicated, but they must be anticipated.

How SWOT Turns Into Strategy

Once these factors become clear, you can design a plan that intentionally prepares you for success. For example:

- Use your natural planning skills to leverage your strengths by preparing lunches and snacks with healthy foods you already like.
- Address and improve weaknesses by establishing a calming nighttime routine that relieves stress and minimizes the likelihood of emotional or convenience snacking.
- Capitalize on opportunities such as meal-planning apps, accountability partners, or supportive friends who can help reinforce your goals.
- Manage threats by planning ahead for high-risk situations—keeping nutritious snacks available at work and deciding in advance how you'll handle food-centered events.

With this approach, dietary changes shift from trying harder to establishing a practical plan that aligns with your energy levels, habits, and environment.

Practical Application: A Small Habit That Can Make a Difference

Instead of revamping your whole diet, begin with one simple new habit: prepare one go-to healthy meal or snack the night before.

That's it. Not full meal prep for the week. Not a new diet. Not buying specialty foods or equipment.

Just preparing a healthy item in advance so it's ready to eat when you need it.

This quick, easy activity can become part of your evening wind-down routine—helping you relax while also supporting your choices for tomorrow.

Why This Habit Works Using the SWOT Framework

- Strengths (Leverage): It leverages existing motivation and planning tendencies.
- Weaknesses (Improve): It diminishes the effects of low evening energy, emotional eating, and last-minute convenience choices.
- Opportunities (Capitalize): It optimizes the use of available resources that won't add extra costs, such as support from others and free online tools.
- Threats (Manage): It helps protect you during busy mornings, stressful workdays, and environments with lots of food.

By moving effort to a calmer moment, you lessen reliance on willpower later—when stress and fatigue peak.

What This Could Look Like in Practice

- Prepare a single serving of overnight oats.
- Pre-cut fruits or vegetables to serve later with yogurt or hummus.
- Divide a balanced leftover meal for tomorrow's lunch.

Small, intentional actions add up to meaningful change. These small steps not only move you forward; they also help you *practice change*. Over time, they build confidence, self-mastery, and trust in your ability to follow through.

It's a great starting point.

Eventually, these small actions can grow into larger ones. You might start cooking more meals at home, packing your lunch and snacks, and relying less on, or eliminating, convenience foods—similar to what we saw GC do in the Introduction. By making it a habit to prepare his meals and bring lunch to work, he lost 30 pounds over six months without striving for perfection—just consistency.

We do it to improve it: This is how planned change works in real life.

Every deliberate change you make—whether it's adopting a small new habit or developing entirely new skills—strengthens your ability to handle future change. Each attempt teaches you something: what works for you, what doesn't, and how to adjust. With each small success, your confidence increases.

Over time, these small wins build into a strong skill set for tackling bigger challenges. That's why the seemingly minor successes are so important. Every planned change you make today supports the larger changes you target for tomorrow.

Pick one small, manageable change. Make it deliberate. Try it out.

That's how meaningful change begins, occurs, and endures a lifetime.

Next Up

Speaking of thinking about what we're thinking, hold that thought.

Module 2: Suspend Preconceptions

Acknowledging that we don't know what we don't know, which means we may have more to learn to achieve our change.

Learning Objectives. By the end of this module, you will be able to:

1. Examine how your default assumptions influence perception, interpretation, and choices, and use practical strategies to broaden your mental toolbox for finding new solutions.
2. Evaluate opportunities for personal growth with a balanced attitude of curiosity and skepticism, deciding when to pursue new ideas and when to avoid unproven strategies.
3. Interpret and apply insights from organizational change—primarily psychological, social, and structural drivers of resistance—to enhance your habits and patterns.
4. Design and implement a practical, evidence-based personal action plan that aligns with your tendencies, working with your mind rather than against it.

What Is It?

We probably have heard phrases like, "There are two sides to every story," "Don't jump to conclusions," "It's not always what it seems," "Keep a beginner's mind," or "If the only tool in your toolbox is a hammer, then every problem you face looks like a nail."

Also commonly heard, especially in the context of organizational behavior, are sayings such as "Think outside the box," "We need a paradigm shift," "Challenge the status quo," or "Let's reimagine what's possible."

These expressions remind us that our judgments, biases, and opinions can hinder learning and growth.

This section builds on the core idea from Module 1. To paraphrase Socrates in his discussion of the Greek maxim "Know Thyself," when we set aside our preconceptions, we recognize what we know and what we don't know, and, importantly for self-improvement, stay curious about what we might learn to our advantage.

Suspending preconceptions involves intentionally avoiding snap judgments based on our ingrained beliefs or biases. It means approaching situations with curiosity and humility, understanding that our current views might not always reflect the truth.

This helps us remain open to new information, even when it challenges our existing beliefs.

Why It Matters

We pick up beliefs from our surroundings. Family, culture, school, workplaces, and daily experiences quietly influence the assumptions we hold. Many of these assumptions may have helped us before, but the problem begins when comfort turns into false certainty. What once protected us can gradually become the very obstacle to growth.

It's human nature to hold on to what feels safe. However, safety can disguise itself as truth, keeping us stuck in routines that no longer help us. Familiarity isn't the same as accuracy. When we mistake one for the other, we shut ourselves off from new viewpoints that could improve our future.

Suspending preconceptions isn't about losing who you are—it's about making room for who you can become.

Crucially, planned personal change requires stepping outside our comfort zone. We free up the necessary mental space for transformative insights by suspending our preconceptions. Open-mindedness means allowing some room, at least temporarily, for new ideas that could help us grow and evolve.

Practical Application

When you come across an idea for change, ask yourself:

- Do I already have a strong opinion about this idea?
- What might I gain by considering this, even if it challenges my opinion?
- What could I lose by clinging to my opinion and staying in my comfort zone?

Consider several self-help topics where you likely have experience and strong opinions, such as stress management, increasing your income, diet, exercise, and goal setting. Did you find yourself thinking, I've read the books, and I already know about that; I tried to change, but it didn't work; or That's not for me?

While these thoughts are common, preconceptions can hinder progress.

A technique: Visualize your judgments, biases, and opinions as pieces of laundry hanging on a clothesline. Keep them visible but suspended and out of reach. Then, with a clear mind, evaluate new ideas with curiosity and balanced skepticism. Distinguish between facts and non-facts shaped by past experiences.

Figure 2.1 Suspending Our Preconceptions Out of Reach

A new diet plan serves as a good example.

Suppose we want to lose weight and improve our nutritional balance. Countless diet plans are available online, in books, and are heavily promoted on social media. Maybe we've already tried one or a few, or know someone who has.

With so many dieting choices, meal plans, and advice—both asked for and unsolicited—about what to eat and drink, how do we begin?

With our preconceptions about dieting and nutrition hanging like laundry on a clothesline, we approach the topic with open minds, ready to learn and, within reason, try something different to achieve our goals. Then, we design a plan tailored to our specific needs, desires, and priorities.

It's crucial to our success that this plan remains ours alone, tailored to achieve what we need or want and rooted in our own reality. *There is no one-size-fits-all solution.*

We follow this framework for all our self-improvement efforts, including altering our daily habits and routines, nutrition, income-generating activities, and physical fitness.

Challenges and Pitfalls

As a preliminary reference point, at the beginning of the Enlightenment, Francis Bacon (1561 - 1626) published *Novum Organum*, which discussed the biases and preconceptions that distort human reasoning. He identified four types of distorting factors he called "idols."[24]

Idols of the Tribe: These biases are inherent to human nature. Our mind "resembles those uneven mirrors which impart their own properties to different objects." We tend to see patterns where none exist, be influenced by emotions, and rely on subjective experiences rather than objective reality.

Idols of the Den: Our experiences, education, and environment shape these biases. We each have our own den or cavern, "which intercepts and corrupts the light of nature." Our minds filter and distort reality based on our backgrounds, interests, and preconceptions.

Idols of the Market: Distortions come from language and communication. Words are powerful but can also be dangerous. For we "converse by means of language, but words are formed by the will of the generality." Ambiguous, imprecise, or misleading words and definitions can lead to misunderstandings and confusion, ultimately resulting in errors in reasoning.

Idols of the Theatre: These errors stem from the grand "stage plays" of philosophy, ideology, and tradition—systems of thought that may seem convincing but often resemble mere performances. They can cause us to accept popular ideas as unquestionable truths. To avoid being misled by these ready-made narratives, we practice rational scrutiny, critically examining even well-respected authorities and traditions through evidence and reason.

So, that's a theory, anyway.

In practice, as with many things in life, letting go of our preconceptions is often easier said than done.

Maintaining a bias-free and open mind can be challenging as we navigate everyday life and pursue personal growth. At the same time, we should be careful about accepting everything as valuable without question.

On one end of the spectrum, we might be completely closed-minded, rejecting all new ideas for self-improvement. On the other end, we could be so open-minded that we impulsively, perhaps out of desperation, adopt anything new we encounter without enough thought.

The following figure illustrates the extremes and the midpoint between the two.

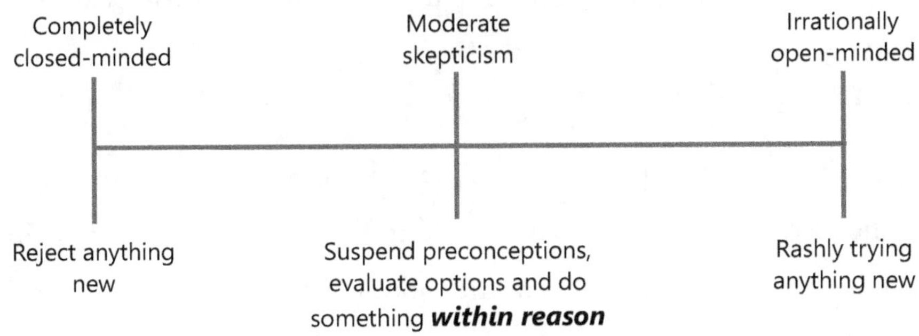

Figure 2.2 Spectrum of Open-Mindedness

Healthy skepticism is essential for self-improvement. Change requires the willingness to learn and possibly try something new, but if something seems too good to be true, it probably is.

While complete certainty isn't always necessary or possible, taking that first step toward change matters. Carefully evaluate new ideas, balancing skepticism with openness. To achieve lasting change, we must step outside our comfort zones. By setting aside our preconceptions, we can explore unfamiliar territory with curiosity and discernment.

It's not about abandoning who we are, but about learning to become more like who we want to be.

As we progress, we'll examine practical tools to tailor our approaches to change based on our individual lives. Whether it's managing stress, finding a new job, improving our diet, getting physically fit, sleeping better, or any other personal goal for self-improvement, the main idea stays the same: Open-mindedness fosters transformation.

Timeless Wisdom

The advice to keep an open, receptive, and curious mind, to acknowledge what we don't know, and to think like a beginner remains as relevant today as it has been throughout history.

As we learn from Japanese Zen monk Shunryu Suzuki, the term *shoshin* in Japan means "beginner's mind." He teaches:[25]

> This does not mean a closed mind, but actually
> an empty mind and a ready mind.
>
> If your mind is empty, it is always ready for
> anything; it is open to everything.
>
> In the beginner's mind, there are many
> possibilities; in the expert's mind there are few.

Professor Mark Muesse explains that thinking like a beginner is grounded in the practice of "not-knowing."[26] Not-knowing doesn't mean abandoning what we already understand or pretending to be un-informed. Instead, it means acknowledging that our current knowledge is incomplete and approaching situations with the openness and curiosity needed to learn what we don't yet see. Not-knowing keeps us flexible, receptive, and eager to gather the information required to move toward our goals

For a classic example, we look to Plato's *Apology*, where Socrates defends himself against charges brought by the Athenians, who accused him of corrupting the youth and opposing the city's gods. Concerning what we know and don't know, in his defense speech, Socrates said:[27]

> Well, although I do not suppose that either of us
> knows anything really beautiful and good, I am
> better off than he is,—for he knows nothing, and
> thinks that he knows; I neither know nor think
> that I know. In this latter particular, then, I seem
> to have slightly the advantage of him.

Socrates argues that he is wiser than the unnamed politician because he recognizes his own ignorance, while the politician falsely believes he knows everything. This passage emphasizes the importance of humility in the pursuit of wisdom.

Before Plato's *Apology*, we look back to Confucius. His advice on ignorance is often summarized as, "To know what you know and what you do not know, that is true knowledge." From the *Confucian Analects,* we find the following passage that's similar in meaning:[28]

> When you know a thing, to hold that you know
> it; and when you do not know a thing, to allow
> that you do not know it—this is knowledge.

Here, Confucius suggests that knowledge involves recognizing the limits of our understanding and, importantly for self-improvement, admitting the areas where we're deficient.

Lastly, we have Lao Tzu and the *Tao Te Ching,* where we learn about what he called the disease of knowing:[29]

> To know and yet think we do not know is the
> highest attainment; not to know and yet think we
> do know is a disease.
>
> It is simply by being pained at the thought of
> having this disease that we are preserved from it.
>
> The sage has not the disease. He knows the pain
> that would be inseparable from it, and therefore
> he does not have it.

This passage on the importance of not-knowing underscores the value of openness to learning while avoiding the dangers of ignorance and arrogance. Lao Tzu stresses that this wisdom helps us navigate life with insight, steering clear of pitfalls that can block or limit our understanding.

Anecdote: Lessons from the South Pole

As a student of military strategy, I learned of two contrasting expeditions to the South Pole that offer valuable lessons on remaining open-minded and receptive to new ideas. To clarify, this discussion is not intended as harsh criticism or praise of either expedition, nor is it merely about "what could have, would have, or should have been." At that time, no one had reached the South Pole, so there was no confirmed practical way to do so.

"Hindsight is 20/20" is often described as having perfect vision when looking back at past events to better understand how certain decisions led to specific outcomes. However, it's important to remember that real-time choices are often made when the "right" approach isn't always clear.

As we know from our own experiences, we might have chosen differently if a clearer option had been available at the moment of decision. This story highlights the difficulties of decision-making in uncertain situations, where clarity only comes after the fact.

It encourages us to reflect without judgment, keep an open mind, and learn from our experiences. With this understanding, we apply relevant lessons to plan for change effectively. Our planning also involves evaluating options to minimize risks, while recognizing that accepting the risks of change is essential, since risk is always present.

In this story, the risks were high.

At the start of the 20th century, two explorers, Robert Falcon Scott from Britain and Roald Amundsen from Norway, both aimed to be the first to reach the South Pole.

Although they set out on their journeys at roughly the same time and had access to similar resources—including skilled team members, animals, modern equipment, and supplies—their results were vastly different.

As Roland Huntford describes in his book, the two expeditions were shaped by their contrasting philosophies of travel, cultural backgrounds, leadership styles, and levels of open-mindedness, all while facing the pressures of national pride.[30]

Scott's team relied on the traditional British approach to polar travel, using a mix of Siberian ponies, experimental motor sledges, and man-hauling—where the men themselves pulled the heavy sledges. The ponies were intended to haul loads early in the journey, but they struggled in the deep snow and extreme cold, and the motor sledges broke down soon after the expedition began.

As a result, Scott's party depended heavily on man-hauling for most of the route. Their clothing, made largely of wool and cotton, offered limited protection in Antarctic conditions. Despite strong evidence that dog teams were the most effective means of polar travel, Scott used them sparingly, remaining committed to his familiar methods and reluctant to adapt to Antarctica's unique demands.

Tragically, when Scott's team reached the South Pole in January 1912, they discovered that Roald Amundsen had arrived over a month earlier. Even more devastating, on their exhausting return trip, Scott and his remaining men fell victim to exhaustion, starvation, and exposure—just 11 miles from a supply depot that might have saved them.

In stark contrast, Amundsen's success stemmed largely from his deep respect for indigenous Arctic knowledge and his willingness to learn, adopt, and refine the Netsilik Inuit's survival techniques. He lived among the Netsilik, studying their methods of travel, clothing, and food preparation in extreme cold. Roland Huntford notes that the Netsilik—one of Canada's most isolated Inuit groups—had generations of experience thriving in polar conditions, and that Amundsen approached them with humility and genuine curiosity.

Applying what he learned, Amundsen built his Antarctic strategy around expertly managed dog teams, avoiding the inefficiencies of man-hauling and the impracticality of ponies on the polar plateau. He and his men wore Inuit-style fur anoraks (hooded pullover jackets), fur-lined boots, and loose-layered clothing that provided superior insulation and moisture control compared to the wool-and-cotton garments used by Scott's party.

In short, Amundsen improved his strategies by being open-minded, learning from the indigenous Arctic people, and applying their timeless insights. He adjusted his methods for travel and survival in the harsh Antarctic environment, allowing his team to reach the Pole first and return home safely.

The different expeditions offer lessons that extend beyond polar exploration. Just as Scott's strict adherence to familiar methods led to disaster, while Amundsen's open-mindedness and adaptability brought success, our personal growth depends on how we face challenges and opportunities and how well we manage risk.

South Pole Lessons for Personal Change

- Challenge Preconceptions: Holding onto familiar methods or past experiences can prevent us from seeing better solutions. Scott's reliance on practices that worked in a different context shows that clinging to old habits or assumptions can impede personal growth.
- Embrace Humility. Amundsen's willingness to live among, study, and learn from the Inuit shows the value of humility. Growth often involves recognizing our limits and seeking insight from new or unconventional sources.
- Prioritize Adaptation. Flexibility is crucial. Just as Amundsen adjusted his strategies to reach the South Pole, personal success depends on our willingness to learn, stay open to change, and adapt our approaches to our unique situations.

When developing a personal growth plan, we often depend on what has worked for us—or others—in the past. The story of the race to the South Pole teaches us to pause, evaluate the current situation, consider new viewpoints, and design a plan tailored to the change we're pursuing.

Takeaways

- Suspending our judgments, opinions, and biases is crucial for learning.
- Using our mental clothesline metaphor, we clear our minds of preconceived notions by recognizing them and temporarily hanging these thoughts outside of our immediate reach.
- The concept of keeping our minds open to allow ongoing learning and personal development is as old as human history and remains just as important today.
- Nothing too much: With an open, receptive mind, we avoid becoming overly accepting, naive, or irrationally embracing every new idea.

End of Module 2 – Reflection and Assessment

The following two sections, a reflection first and then a self-assessment, can help us better identify where preconceptions might hinder progress when making planned personal changes.

Reflection: Resisting Change

Terms and phrases used in modern organizational behavior theory to describe resistance to change, such as habit, fear of the unknown, selective perception, vague communication, or groupthink, can be mapped onto Francis Bacon's four idols.

Over the centuries, language and phrasing have evolved. Still, the main idea stays the same: human minds, whether working alone or in groups, distort reality in predictable ways, which can lead to resistance to change.

Below is a summary that connects current ideas and strategies for resisting change to Bacon's framework, illustrating that "new" insights often reinforce timeless truths.

Idols of the Tribe: Biases Common to All Humans

Errors that naturally occur from being human—typical tendencies in perception and reasoning.

Modern Concepts Corresponding to Idols of the Tribe:

- Fear of the unknown: A natural human tendency to favor the familiar, avoid uncertainty, and overestimate potential losses.

- Cognitive biases: Confirmation bias (seeking information to confirm one's existing beliefs or expectations), loss aversion (avoiding losses more than seeking equivalent gains—losses feel worse than gains feel good), and status quo bias (preferring the current state even when better options are available) all echo Bacon's warning that the mind sees what it wants and resists disconfirming evidence.

- Overgeneralization or pattern-seeking: Employees or leaders might assume "this change will fail because the last one did" by projecting past patterns onto the current situation.

Idols of the Den (or, Cave): Individual Biases

Errors that are influenced by each person's background, habits, and environment.

Modern Concepts Corresponding to Idols of the Den:

- Habit: Each person lives in a "den" shaped by their unique experiences, preferences, and mental tendencies. In modern terms, habits and routines operate in similar ways. They simplify decision-making but also narrow perception, restrict creativity, and make us and our organizations resistant to new ideas. What feels familiar becomes what feels true, even when better options are available.

- Threats to expertise: Specialists, shaped by their training and experience, may resist changes that threaten the value of their hard-won knowledge. This limited perspective leads to defensive reactions and increases resistance to organizational change.

- Selective information processing: Each of us interprets the world through a private mental "den"—our temperament, background, and ingrained ways of thinking. These personal filters shape what we notice and trust. In organizations, they can align into shared "echo chambers," where individual distortions compound into collective narratives that feel true simply because they are familiar.

Idols of the Market: Distortions from Language

Errors caused by misleading, vague, or emotionally charged words.

Modern Concepts Corresponding to Idols of the Market:

- Communication can be hindered when leaders use vague terms like efficiency, innovation, or synergy without clear definitions, which can cause confusion and mistrust.

- Rumors and misinformation: Vague or unclear messages encourage speculation, which fuels resistance.

- Framing effects: How change is described, such as restructuring versus downsizing, can influence acceptance or resistance.

Idols of the Theatre: Dogmas from Philosophical Systems

Organizations often choose to stick with rigid systems or scripts rather than engage critically with reality.

Modern Concepts Corresponding to Idols of the Theater:

- Groupthink: Like actors on stage following a script, organizations suppress dissent and stick to dominant narratives, stopping new perspectives from emerging.
- Tradition as Dogma: "This is the way we've always done it" becomes an unquestioned belief, with established processes seen as sacred.
- Resource Defenses: It's often an uncomfortable truth that the people blocking change may be those with the most authority. Power, budgets, and authorities are seen as fixed roles in a script that must not be changed. Efforts to alter these structures don't just face routine organizational resistance; they often encounter fierce pushback from the most senior and well-positioned leaders whose influence depends on maintaining the status quo. This makes resource reform one of the most challenging types of change. It's not the people, but their leaders.

The following table summarizes comparisons between Bacon's idols and modern organizational change management (OCM) concepts, illustrating the psychological, social, and structural factors that affect resistance to and the success of change initiatives.

Modern Concept	Idol	Explanation / Connection	Modern Concept	Idol	Explanation / Connection
Fear of the unknown	Tribe	Humans naturally prefer the familiar and exaggerate risks of uncertainty.	Ambiguous communication	Market	Vague or imprecise terms confuse employees and make change harder to accept.
Cognitive biases	Tribe	The human mind tends to distort reality, seeing what it wants to see and clinging to stability.	Rumors and misinformation	Market	Unclear language creates space for distortion, speculation, and misunderstanding.
Over-generalizing past events	Tribe	People project past failures or successes onto present situations, perceiving false patterns.	Framing Effects	Market	How a change is worded can alter how it is accepted and supported, or not.
Habit	Den	Personal routines create comfort; individuals resist disrupting the patterns of their "den."	Groupthink	Theatre	Conformity to a dominant "script"; dissent and inquiry are suppressed.
Threats to expertise	Den	Specialists may resist change if it undermines the value of their hard-won skills or knowledge base.	Institutional resistance / Security in tradition	Theatre	"The way we've always done it" — norms defended as unquestionable truths.
Selective information processing	Den	Individuals notice or accept only data that fits prior beliefs, ignoring conflicting evidence.	Threat to established resource allocation	Theatre	Organizational actors see their power and allocations as fixed, like having permanent roles in a play.

Table 2.1 Bacon's Idols and OCM Concepts

Self-Assessment: Suspend Preconceptions

When we aim for a planned personal change—such as reducing stress, finding a better or first job, losing weight, or starting a new fitness routine—our minds don't always work in our favor.

Preconceptions, habits, and emotional reactions can shape how you interpret options and evidence. One of the biggest challenges in self-improvement is learning to pause these automatic thoughts long enough to consider new, potentially better approaches.

Philosopher Francis Bacon referred to these distortions as the "idols of the mind."

These are patterns of bias that come from human nature, personal experience, everyday language, and cultural scripts. Recognizing and suspending these distortions can help you think more clearly about stress management, career decisions, health, and other life changes.

How to Use This Sheet

Identify a specific, meaningful, and achievable personal change you plan to pursue.

What do you already know about making this change? A helpful starting point is your SWOT analysis from Module 1, which highlights your strengths, weaknesses, opportunities, and threats related to this specific change.

What other information might you need, or what could you compare, before you commit to a plan?

As you work through the following questions, try to suspend your preconceptions. This isn't about judging yourself but about making room for a clearer understanding.

This reflection is just for you. It's designed to help you identify biases, assumptions, comfort zones, vague language, or outside authority that might influence your decisions.

With greater self-awareness, you can develop a more informed, evidence-based action plan.

The Four Idols

1. Idols of the Tribe: Biases Common to All Humans

Errors caused by natural human tendencies in perception and reasoning.

For the change I'm considering:

- Am I trusting an idea because it feels familiar and comfortable, rather than because it is effective?
- How might my current emotions—stress, excitement, fear—be influencing my perception of this choice?
- What objective evidence supports my thinking? If I rely solely on intuition, how can I test it safely before making a commitment?

2. Idols of the Den: Individual Biases

Biases are influenced by personal experiences, habits, and environment.

For the change I want to make:

- How might my upbringing or past experiences affect my expectations or fears?
- Am I ignoring an option just because it's unfamiliar or doesn't match my usual ways?
- How might someone with a vastly different background see this same decision—and what can I learn from their perspective?

3. Idols of the Market: Distortions from Language

Errors caused by vague, misleading, or emotionally charged words.

For my specific goal:

- Am I using broad terms like healthy, successful, or balanced without clearly defining what they mean specifically for me?
- How can I rephrase my goal in clear, practical, and measurable terms that fit my situation?
- Am I more influenced by slogans, online chatter, or buzzwords than by evidence and reasoning?

4. Idols of the Theatre: Dogmas from Systems and Traditions

Mistakes that arise from adopting popular frameworks, trends, or one-size-fits-all solutions.

For the change I'm contemplating:

- Am I relying on a popular plan or method just because it's trendy or commonly accepted?
- What assumptions am I making simply because "everyone says so"?
- How can I safely test this method or belief in my own life to see if it works for me?

Example: Using SWOT Analysis with Idols When Considering Entering the Job Market as a High School or College Graduate

Scenario: You've finished high school or college and aren't sure which path to take next. Your options include:

- Taking a job locally.
- Moving far away for a seemingly better opportunity.
- Joining the military.
- Returning to school (trade school, transitioning from high school to college, obtaining additional certifications, or moving from college to a graduate program).

You've completed a SWOT analysis, but the choices still feel overwhelming. This is a perfect moment to pause, suspend preconceptions, and walk through the four idols.

1. Idols of the Tribe: Universal Human Biases

How these might show up:

- We often overvalue immediate comfort and undervalue long-term benefits.
- We tend to believe the path others choose is the "normal" one.
- Strong emotions like fear of change or excitement about independence can cloud judgment.

Using your SWOT:

- Your strengths may include adaptability and curiosity, but fear, a common bias, might cause you to overlook those strengths and choose the "safe" option—accepting the local job.
- Your opportunities, like the chance to build independence and grow through challenge, might feel far away compared to the comfort of staying home.

Questions to help suspend these biases:

- Am I choosing the most familiar path because it feels safe, not because it aligns with my strengths and long-term goals?
- Is my fear of leaving home a short-term feeling that's overshadowing long-term opportunities?

2. Idols of the Den: Personal, Experience-Based Biases

How these might show up:

- Your upbringing or community might emphasize stability, or conversely, may view college as "the only respectable" option.

- If you were raised around military family members, you might be biased for or against that choice.
- Past successes or failures could make you overconfident or hesitant.

Using your SWOT:

- Your weaknesses might include limited work experience, which could make certain options either a good fit or a poor match. For example, the structure and clear guidance of the military or a well-organized academic program could benefit someone who is capable but still building practical career skills.
- At the same time, this limitation could make a distant move, an unstructured college path, or demanding roles feel overwhelming or poorly suited to your current level of readiness.
- Your threats might include local job scarcity or limited support if you move far away. However, these could seem exaggerated if you've always been warned against taking big risks.

Questions to help suspend these biases:

- Which of my reactions are my own, and which are influenced by family expectations or local norms?
- If someone with a different background had my same strengths and opportunities, how might they perceive this choice differently?

3. Idols of the Market: Language-Driven Distortions

How these might show up:

- Phrases and words like good job, risky, secure, stable career, or failure can carry strong emotional weight without being clearly defined.
- Buzzwords from social media or peers—hustle, grind, gap year, stability, purpose—may influence you toward certain paths without thorough analysis.

Using your SWOT:

- Your strengths and opportunities will become much clearer once you replace vague terms with specific, personal definitions.
- When you define "stable career" for yourself, for example, you might realize that the safe option, like going back to school immediately, could actually be less aligned with your strengths or more financially risky than you thought.

Questions to help suspend these biases:

- What do "good job," "big risk," or "success" specifically mean to me—not to my parents, friends, or what I see on social media?
- If I rewrite each option in clear, measurable terms, such as salary range, career development, stability, physical demands, and time commitment, does my preference change?

4. Idols of the Theatre: Scripts, Systems, and Common Wisdom

How these might show up:

- The idea that you must go to college to succeed, or the opposite belief that college is a waste unless it guarantees a job, can seem like unquestioned truths.

- Military recruitment campaigns, university advertising, and cultural stories about adventure or responsibility often come across as familiar scripts.

Using your SWOT:

- Compare each option against your SWOT analysis instead of cultural scripts.

- If discipline and structure are weaknesses, the military's script of "we'll make you stronger" may seem appealing, but military life could become overwhelming.

- If your strengths include self-direction and curiosity, the script that says "just take whatever job you can find" might greatly hinder your growth.

Questions to help suspend these biases:

- Am I leaning toward or away from an option just because it fits a popular story or identity—the responsible student, the adventurous one, the loyal hometown kid, the one who makes something of themselves?

- How can I test each path with small actions, like job shadowing, talking to former service members, informational interviews, or campus visits, to see if the narrative really matches reality?

Putting It All Together

After reviewing your SWOT and considering each idol with a clearer mind, you might come to conclusions such as:

- I'm debating whether to stay with the local job that feels 'safe,' but my strengths in learning and adaptability suggest staying could keep me stuck. Or, I initially thought I needed to move to grow, but my strong community ties and local opportunities better match my skills than uprooting myself.

- I used to see moving far away as 'risky,' but once I clearly defined the risks, I saw the opportunity aligns well with my strengths and long-term goals. Or, I imagined that moving would be exciting and life-changing, but when I examined the risks, I realized I'd be taking on financial and emotional strain that don't really fit my current strengths or objectives.

- I came to understand that I was more attracted to the idea of joining the military than to its daily realities. Or, initially, I dismissed the military as too rigid, but after examining the facts beyond the stereotypes, I realized that its structure, training, and clear career paths could be the ideal environment for me to thrive.

- Returning to school sounds exciting, but I realize I need real-world work experience first. Or, I was worried that going back to school might delay starting real life, but I've discovered that my best career opportunities come from gaining more training and education now, before I incur obligations that might limit my options later.

The goal is not to select the "right" option immediately; rather, it is to choose intentionally, not out of fear, vague language, or inherited scripts.

This training program offers much more to explore in personal transformation, but honest reflection like this is essential for self-mastery. Since life inevitably requires us to take risks, it's helpful to remember that the instincts we rely on are strengthened by the self-knowledge we gain here.

Next Up

Focusing our efforts where it matters most.

Module 3: Focus on Control

If you can't do anything about it, don't worry about it.—Jeanne Calment, verified as the world's longest-living person.[31]

Learning Objectives. By the end of this module, you will be able to:

1. Differentiate between what you can control, influence, and what is beyond both.
2. Use strategies to focus on factors you can control—your thoughts, choices, and actions—and act intentionally within your sphere of influence to shape your environment and guide others.
3. Assess challenges beyond your control and influence, and seek appropriate support to protect your wellbeing while working toward your goals.

What Is It?

We gain control over our self-improvement when we stop chasing external things and focus on mastering what is within us. In self-mastery, control means guiding our attention to our thoughts, choices, and actions. It is through these inner resources that personal change and lifelong growth unfold.

Equally important is recognizing what is beyond our control: external circumstances, other people's opinions or actions, and many of life's outcomes. Accepting these limits frees us from pointless struggle and helps us focus our energy on what matters.

Areas we can control include:

- Our thoughts—how we interpret situations.
- Our choices—the actions we take each day, big or small.
- Our time and effort—where we focus our energy.
- Our learning—how we respond to mistakes and pursue growth.
- Our social interactions—who we spend time with.
- Our goals—setting realistic and meaningful objectives.

By anchoring ourselves in these areas, we gain clarity, resilience, and a stronger sense of agency. The shift from trying to control the uncontrollable to mastering ourselves is where we foster lasting growth.

Why It Matters

Life feels lighter and more empowering when we stop resisting what we can't change and instead focus on what we can, like our thoughts, choices, attitudes, and habits. While we can't control the world around us, we can always control how we think, what we learn, and the goals we pursue.

Focusing our energy on what we can control boosts confidence and a sense of ownership. Every deliberate decision—how we spend our time, how we prioritize our efforts, what we commit to—strengthens our ability to achieve meaningful change. This feeling of agency builds momentum and encourages us to take consistent steps toward our goals.

Focusing on what we can control also shields us from unnecessary stress. When we let go of attachment to outcomes and the actions of others, we open up mental and emotional space for what matters in our growth. This clarity not only reduces anxiety but also allows us to use our limited resources—time, energy, money, and attention—more effectively.

By mastering what is within us rather than being overwhelmed by what lies outside, we build resilience, purpose, and confidence to face life's challenges.

Practical Application

Regarding self-help, the following figure illustrates three perspectives on pursuing our planned personal change.

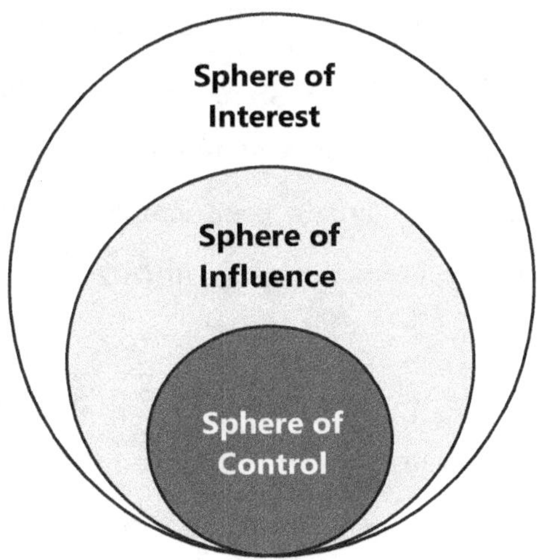

Figure 3.1 The Spheres of Interest, Influence, and Control

Sphere of Interest

Starting from the outermost sphere, with an open and curious mind, we explore ideas, tools, and techniques related to our change within our area of interest. This includes those things that grab our attention: published research and reports, books, websites, podcasts, social media posts, and casual conversations.

This outer sphere is enormous—a vast ocean of information, research, conflicting commentary, opinions, distractions, and loud noise to navigate. Some of it can inform or inspire our progress, but we must intentionally engage with it. Looking ahead, in Module 6: Prove It to Yourself, we explore ways to navigate this seemingly endless sea. Importantly, we spend enough time in our sphere of interest to identify what's relevant, analyze what matters, determine what's valuable to us in our specific situation, and then take action accordingly.

The more time we spend aimlessly drifting—scrolling, debating, overthinking, or worrying—the less energy we have to change behaviors that promote progress. Sustainable change involves shifting from merely consuming information to actually producing results. However, moving away from being only a consumer of information can be particularly challenging.

Here's a clear example of how self-awareness can be your ally. As you explore your sphere of interest, notice where you focus. Ask yourself: Does my time and effort here support the change I need or want to make—or does it just keep me busy? Am I impulsively chasing clickbait?

As the saying goes, don't confuse activity with progress.

Progress often involves letting go of what's irrelevant or distracting. Reclaiming focus is an act of strength. When you shift your time and attention inward— from what merely interests you to what you can control or influence—you regain momentum.

Sphere of Influence

When we move inward from the vast array of things that grab our attention, we enter our sphere of influence. In this space, we can influence outcomes, shape conditions, and interact with and affect the people around us, even though we can't directly control them.

You've already gone through this many times: convincing a family member, encouraging a friend, classmate, or coworker, or setting up your home to support a habit you want to change. Influence feels familiar, even if we rarely take the time to study it.

Within our sphere of influence, we can share ideas, motivate others, and adapt our environment to support our self-improvement efforts. Through communication, collaboration, and consistent actions, we can often inspire change or guide situations toward the goals that matter to us.

But our influence has its limits.

We can't control others' choices or how our environment responds. Sometimes, even with genuine effort, change doesn't happen.

Recognizing this limit is both humbling and freeing. It reminds us that our energy is valuable—and that meaningful progress occurs when we focus it where it can make a difference.

This is another thing we know firsthand. Whether as parents, grandparents, siblings, teachers, bosses, coworkers, classmates, or friends, we've all felt the gap between what *we* want and expect others to do and what *they* ultimately choose to do.

This might be the first interaction in history, dating back to when the first two humans faced each other and both wondered: How can I get that other person to do what I want?

In Phase One, we learn to develop self-mastery through inward-focused tools and practices for intentional personal growth—while recognizing that meaningful progress rarely occurs in isolation. Even the strongest internal work exists within a broader context.

Our habits, routines, decisions, and intentions are constantly shaped by the world around us—our relationships, physical spaces, and the systems we move through each day. No matter how disciplined or motivated we become, lasting change partly depends on how well our external environment supports those efforts.

Phase Two shifts our focus outward to understand and navigate the external environment. Instead of relying solely on willpower, we begin exploring how the conditions around us influence behavior, momentum, and opportunities, and how to plan for our change accordingly.

As an introduction to acting within our sphere of influence, we refer to the Army's strategic concept of *shaping the environment*—the notion that success involves not only responding to situations but also, whenever possible, intentionally influencing them in advance. Applied to personal growth, this perspective shows how small, purposeful changes to our surroundings can set the conditions for easier, more lasting change.

Shaping the Environment: Setting the Conditions for Success

In the U.S. Army's operational framework outlined in *Field Manual (FM) 3-0: Operations*, "shaping the environment" refers to actions that establish favorable conditions, mitigate risks, and influence perceptions and behaviors before crises emerge.[32] These operations are proactive rather than reactive, aiming to set the conditions for future success by building trust, strengthening partnerships, and deterring threats without conflict.

At the strategic level, shaping can include joint training with allies, humanitarian outreach, or forward deployments that demonstrate readiness and promote stability. The message is clear: by shaping the operational environment early, the Army prepares to respond effectively when challenges arise.

Just like the Army intentionally shapes its operational environment to foster stability and success, we can use the same approach in our own lives. In self-improvement, "shaping our environment" means taking purposeful, proactive actions that make the desired changes easier and help prevent setbacks.

Whether our goal is to reduce stress, advance our careers, or improve our diet, exercise, or sleep, we can strengthen our position by laying a solid foundation. This might include organizing our physical space to reduce friction, building supportive networks, refining routines, or setting clear boundaries.

Similar to the Army's strategic shaping operations, our efforts to influence others and/or change our environment don't guarantee results. However, they inform us about what we're facing, reduce uncertainty, expand our options, and better prepare us for success.

As we'll explore in depth in Phase Two, shaping our environment means deliberately engineering the conditions that make growth easier and setbacks less costly. It's not about controlling everything—because we can't—but about identifying what can be shaped and taking responsibility for those levers. When the environment supports your goals, change stops relying on willpower alone and starts becoming sustainable.

Examples of Shaping Your Environment

Our careers: We can shape our professional landscape by actively networking and staying prepared for the changing job market. This involves staying aware of industry trends, engaging in continuous learning, and upskilling as economic conditions change. By taking these proactive steps, we increase our access to opportunities and stay relevant, much like forward deployments ensure readiness in operational regions.

Diet and Exercise: We can boost our health by removing junk food from our pantry and keeping workout clothes visible as reminders to follow our exercise routine. Surrounding ourselves with people who prioritize health is also helpful. These small logistical steps and daily actions make it easier to reach our health goals.

Sleep Quality: While we can't eliminate every stressor, we can modify our environment to reduce its effects. Setting a regular bedtime, dimming the lights, quieting our surroundings, putting away our phones, and establishing a consistent evening wind-down routine are all effective methods. These proactive steps help us rest and recover properly.

Shaping our environment requires foresight and planning. Just as the Army invests in stability to prevent conflict, we can invest in structure, boundaries, and habits that help prevent burnout, indecision, and regret. Although we cannot control every variable, we can influence the systems that support our efforts to achieve positive change.

Sphere of Control

Finally, at the core of our framework is the sphere of control—our most dependable source of power in self-improvement. Here, we alone choose our thoughts, how we respond to external events, and how we prepare for the change we want to make.

As you plan for your specific change, pay attention to where your focus naturally shifts. Are you drifting into the sphere of interest? Are you unsuccessfully trying to persuade, correct, or reorganize others within your sphere of influence? Or are you first redirecting your attention back to what you can fully control—your own thoughts, choices, and actions?

Self-improvement centers on what we can control and deliberately influence in our environment.

In short: Control "P" and influence "E"

By doing this, we improve our ability to plan for and achieve meaningful change while avoiding the frustration and distraction of focusing on what is beyond our reach. From this perspective, even small, steady steps can lead to significant, lasting change.

For self-improvement, some things we can control include our:

- Thoughts: We can choose how we respond to situations and interpret events. For example, instead of thinking, "I always fail," we can reframe our thoughts to, "I can learn and use this knowledge to help myself improve."
- Choices: Our daily actions are within our control. This might mean committing to healthier habits, such as cooking at home instead of eating out or dedicating time each day to exercise, even if it's just a short walk.
- Time Management: A universal factor affects everyone equally—no matter who we are, where we live, or our circumstances: we all have 24 hours in a day. That's all we get, so it's important to use

our time wisely. By setting priorities and following schedules, we can increase productivity and reduce stress.

- Learning and Growth: Our commitment to personal development is within our control. This can involve seeking educational resources, attending workshops, or simply dedicating time to reading to acquire new skills or relevant knowledge.

- Social Interactions: Choosing supportive, respectful, and energizing relationships boosts our emotional wellbeing, while establishing healthy boundaries with draining or harmful interactions protects our focus, reduces stress, and maintains stability.

- Goals: We set our goals carefully to ensure they are realistic and align with our values. For example, to get fit, we might aim to walk an extra 15 minutes each day, setting a clear, measurable, and manageable target.

Challenges and Pitfalls

Personal growth involves taking full responsibility for self-improvement. Change starts from within: focus on what we can control and commit to measurable progress. While self-reliance is crucial, it's also important to recognize when we need support.

Often, growth doesn't happen in isolation; mentors, professionals, and trusted others can offer valuable insights, fill knowledge gaps, and help us navigate career, physical, and mental health challenges. However, as we've seen, asking for help doesn't guarantee we will receive it. We can seek guidance or cooperation, but others' willingness or ability to help, and how much they do, is beyond our control.

Similarly, while we can influence change in some areas of our environment, most external factors will be beyond our reach. And crucially, fixating on what we cannot change only hinders our progress.

Sustainable self-improvement comes from consistently focusing on what we can control—our thoughts, choices, and actions—and actively working to shape our environment as much as possible. This approach sets the stage for meaningful growth and development by building resilience and adaptability.

Balancing personal responsibility with the wisdom to seek help and recognizing the limits of external influence helps us set a path that is both realistic and empowering.

Another common issue involves the word "control," which appears in many different contexts. To prevent confusion, let's briefly review how this term might be used in other ways.

Clarifying "Control" in Self-Help Versus Other Contexts

In this training program, we use the term control in the self-help sense: it is inward-focused. Control involves managing your thoughts, deciding how to respond, and shaping your personal habits and routines.

Influence, on the other hand, is outward-focused—how you engage with and shape your environment and relationships, and how you leverage opportunities to achieve your goals. You can't control external events; you can only influence them to some degree.

It's worth noting that other fields use the word differently. For one example, in the Army's operational context, command and control

(C2) refers to the authority leaders have to direct forces, make decisions, coordinate actions, and ensure a mission unfolds as intended.[33] Here, control is hierarchical, externally focused, and immediate. It involves coordinating people and resources to reach a goal in a complex environment—not managing emotions or personal development.

While the Army, for example, uses control to mean coordinating and directing external activities, in self-improvement, we use it to refer to managing what happens internally, where we alone hold complete power.

Timeless Wisdom

Once again, we look to examples in our rich written history to remind us to focus on what we can control in our self-improvement efforts.

Stephen Covey introduced the concept of circles of concern and influence in his 1989 book, *The 7 Habits of Highly Effective People*. He presented this idea in the context of developing proactivity, which is his first habit. Covey encourages us to recognize our power to choose our responses and focus on areas where we can make meaningful differences.[34]

Before that, in 1966, psychologist Julian Rotter introduced the concept of "locus of control" to help explain how we perceive the connection between our actions and their outcomes.[35] Having an internal locus of control means we tend to believe that our efforts, choices, and talents directly affect our outcomes. From this perspective, we see personal success or failure as something we can shape, which motivates us to adjust our actions to achieve our goals.

On the other hand, when we have an external locus of control, we often believe that events occur because of luck, fate, chance, other people's decisions, or environmental factors. This perspective can lead us to view personal change as largely beyond our control, making it harder to find the motivation to implement the changes we need or want.

Rotter didn't claim that one view is right and the other wrong. Instead, he highlighted that our beliefs about control are fundamental. These beliefs shape how we handle challenges, recover from setbacks, and continue pursuing our needs and wants.

Crucially, our locus of control is not fixed; we can change it. When we believe our actions have even a slight impact on achieving our goals, we gain greater power to shape our lives.

For an earlier reference, Reinhold Niebuhr, an American theologian, is often credited with writing *The Serenity Prayer* in the early 1930s. It gained popularity through Alcoholics Anonymous (AA), and they continue to recite it to this day. Here is AA's abbreviated version:[36]

> God grant me the serenity to
> accept the things I cannot change,
> courage to change the things I can,
> and wisdom to know the difference.

This prayer reminds us to acknowledge the limits of our influence and encourages us to focus on changing what can be changed.

Finally, we mention two well-known Stoic philosophers from ancient Rome and Greece: Marcus Aurelius, the Roman emperor who lived from 121 to 180 CE, and Epictetus, born a Greek slave and later freed, who lived from 55 to 135 CE.

Marcus Aurelius describes the "rational soul" as our ability for reason and self-awareness, while the "ruling faculty" manages our judgments and decisions. These ideas are central to Stoic philosophy, which teaches that wellbeing results not from external events but from how we exercise reason through virtue.

In *Meditations*, Marcus Aurelius considers the rational soul a part of the divine Logos within human nature. Influenced by Epictetus, he advises himself to maintain inner harmony, act justly, and stay undisturbed by external factors and events. He writes:[37]

> These are the properties of the rational soul:
> it sees itself, analyses itself, and makes itself
> such as it chooses; the fruit which it bears
> itself enjoys.

Regarding the ruling faculty, he reminds us:[38]

> If thou art pained by any external thing,
> it is not this thing that disturbs thee,
> but thy own judgment about it. And it is
> in thy power to wipe out this judgment now.

> Remember that the ruling faculty is invincible,
> when self-collected it is satisfied with itself,
> if it does nothing which it does not choose
> to do, even if it resist from mere obstinacy.

Our rational soul has a faculty that functions as the center of judgment and perception. This faculty is self-aware and reflective, enabling us to shape our inner world. We can analyze our thoughts, make adjustments, and build inner strength.

An external event is neither inherently good nor bad; it is only our judgment that assigns it value.

Recognizing this, we regulate our emotional state and foster resilience and personal growth. This self-awareness helps us approach life's challenges with wisdom and calmness. Marcus Aurelius emphasizes the importance of personal agency and inner strength. His wisdom motivates us to empower ourselves, urging us to master our thoughts and develop our character instead of wasting energy on what is beyond our control.

For Epictetus, the "rational faculty"—especially our ability to make judgments and moral choices—defines what it means to be human and is the foundation of true freedom. In *The Discourses of Epictetus*, he describes this ability as the capacity to reflect on ourselves and distinguish between what is within our control and what is not.[39] This awareness allows us to align our will with reason and the natural order of things.

Epictetus highlights the significance of reason alongside the Stoic principle known as the "dichotomy of control," which he discusses in *The Enchiridion* (The Manual), drawing from *The Discourses.*[40] He teaches that we can control our judgments, desires, and actions to pursue or avoid certain things, but external events and others' actions are beyond our control. Embracing what we cannot control as it happens is the key to peace.

From Marcus Aurelius and Epictetus, we learn to:

- Clearly identify what is within our control and what is not.
- Respond wisely by focusing on what can be changed and accepting the rest calmly.
- Maintain inner peace by letting go of irrational fears, passions, and worries about the unchangeable.

Anecdote: Control, Influence, and the Fine Art of Leadership

This self-help book explores how to achieve the personal change we plan. Informed by self-awareness and guided by self-mastery, we manage ourselves and strategically influence what we can to meet our needs and fulfill our desires. That's empowering.

However, as we saw earlier, there may be times when we need and should seek help from others to pursue our goals—such as career counselors, mentors, specialized trainers and coaches, and medical professionals—while keeping in mind that it is, and always will be, our sole responsibility to pursue and achieve our change.

And then there's the most important step many of us will take in our careers: assuming a leadership role. Building on the earlier discussion in this module about shaping our environment to reduce stress or improve our diet, exercise, or sleep, at some point in our lifelong development, we will likely be asked or, due to circumstances, be compelled to take on an assigned leadership role in the workplace or another formal setting. It is here that we often realize, with startling clarity, the clear boundary between our spheres of control and influence.

Over the years, I've seen many people avoid taking that crucial step into the sphere of influence to lead others. Some never want the responsibility. Others wait too long, hesitating until the opportunity passes by. Or, some try once but pull back when the weight of the role feels heavier than they expected. Others might say they want a front-office role but are unwilling to pay their dues by starting in lower-level positions first.

For many, the deterrent is obvious: leading others can be a stressful role.

Being assigned as a team leader, first-line supervisor, or manager means being responsible for others' productivity, managing resistance, admitting mistakes, and handling the pressure of expectations. It can be nerve-racking and isolating. You're in charge and must answer for the team.

And yet, this same test offers something invaluable. Leadership pushes us beyond our comfort zones, sharpens our judgment, and builds our resilience. It provides the chance to influence outcomes greater than ourselves, to help others grow, and to leave a mark that endures long after the stress has passed.

While leadership theory can be taught, understanding and appreciating what people do—or fail to do—in the workplace comes only through experience. And to gain that experience, we have to practice it.

Leadership is challenging, yet it remains one of the most powerful drivers of growth we will encounter. Since leadership is essential for success in many careers, we'll briefly explore it here in the context of applying self-mastery to better distinguish between our spheres of control and influence.

From Being Led to Leading

Like every Soldier, I had to earn many promotions on time to stay in the Army for a full career. The system was unforgiving—move up or move out. Early promotions came almost automatically, but by the time I reached the threshold for Sergeant, the competition grew fierce. Advancement was no longer about time served; it was about proving myself against peers who wanted it just as badly.

That's when I learned the often-repeated truth I've carried ever since: what got you here won't get you there.

I pushed myself to improve, grow, and compete, eventually earning the right to pin on my Sergeant stripes—still one of the proudest moments in both of my careers.

But with that step came a new reality: for the first time, I wasn't just being led. I was the one leading. I'll never forget standing in front of my newly assigned squad. Some were older, some more experienced, and at that moment, the weight of leadership hit me. My rank gave me authority—but not influence. My drive and ambition weren't enough to inspire them. And I quickly realized I couldn't order people into caring.

With that promotion to Sergeant, I learned the difficult truth: taking on a leadership role is about more than just self-control. It also requires influence—and, most importantly, accountability.

Leadership as the Momentous Step Beyond Control

Over the years, I have encountered numerous definitions of leadership. Many of these highlight the term "influence". Early on, I began to shape my own understanding, starting with:

Leadership is the art of influencing others.

That much is true, but influencing others to do what?

As a newly promoted "buck Sergeant," I learned that influence without clear direction achieves little. In formal frontline roles, leadership becomes genuine when we inspire others to collaborate toward shared, meaningful goals. So, my definition expanded to include:

Leadership is the art of influencing others to achieve common goals through clear objectives.

But that didn't completely reflect my experience with leadership.

The hardest lesson I learned—and one I didn't fully understand or appreciate until I took on my first frontline leadership role—was that leadership also means being personally responsible for what others do, or fail to do. When your team succeeds, it's their victory. When they stumble, it's on you. My definition then expanded to:

Leadership is the art of influencing others to achieve common goals through clear objectives, and being personally responsible for what they do or fail to do.

That final piece—being personally responsible—is what turns influence into leadership.

We can influence others without taking responsibility for their results. That's easier. But we cannot lead others without accepting accountability for what they do or don't do. That's harder.

Leadership demands accountability; influence alone isn't sufficient. That's what makes leadership both challenging and rewarding—effective, accountable leaders are, and always will be, highly sought after in the workplace.

The truth is simple yet profound: leadership isn't about control. We only control ourselves—our thoughts, choices, and actions. Leadership is about genuinely motivating others to do their best in their work and taking responsibility for what gets accomplished—and what doesn't.

· In my first leadership role, I learned that my performance was judged not by my individual work but by the achievements of those I led. I also quickly realized that authority alone doesn't motivate people. True leadership is built through setting an example, providing clarity, offering encouragement, and ensuring accountability.

Another lesson learned was that each team member has a unique motivation style. Some are highly self-motivated and thrive with a clear vision, well-defined objectives, and a level of independence. Others need clear structure, guidance, and more direct encouragement. An effective leader's skill is the ability to adapt—supporting the first group while guiding the second to exceed their own expectations.

Leadership tests your patience, humility, and courage. But it also offers what might be the greatest reward in a career: seeing others succeed because of your influence. When someone on your team grows, achieves, or believes more in themselves because of your guidance, you realize that leadership isn't about position or power. It's about people.

And it's one of the most meaningful journeys you can experience.

Leadership relies on motivation: our own, which we completely control, and others', which we can influence to some degree.

No book, theory, or amount of training can replace the lived experience of leading others. But with each step into greater responsibility, we gain resilience, perspective, and the ability to make an impact far greater than ourselves.

This is the fine art of influencing others.

Influence involves leading by example, listening, connecting goals to a shared mission, and earning trust through respect. Over time, I realized that the stripes on my collar didn't make me a leader; my ability to influence did.

The Army taught me an important lesson early on, which I've come to understand applies to all areas of life—whether in the workplace, at home, in social settings, or within our communities. Effective leadership relies on self-control and is demonstrated through the ability to influence others. While we cannot control others' decisions, we can shape an environment that encourages them to perform at their best.

Our leadership journey begins when we intentionally step beyond what we can control and take personal responsibility in our sphere of influence.

There, in the heat of experience, leaders are forged.

Takeaways

- Our sphere of interest can provide valuable insights as we learn and grow, but ultimately, we need to shift from just consuming information to actively making change.
- Within our sphere of influence, we can somewhat shape our environment to support our self-improvement efforts.
- Our sphere of influence provides valuable leadership opportunities in the workplace and other settings, which are essential for career growth. For many, this represents a significant shift from focusing

solely on our sphere of control to actively engaging within our sphere of influence through leadership roles.

- Within our sphere of control, we hold full power over our thoughts, choices, and actions in pursuit of what we need or want to change.

- Focusing on what we can control empowers us to take responsibility for our self-improvement while preventing frustration and stress from overthinking what we cannot change.

- Nothing too much: While we focus on what we can control and strategically influence in our self-help efforts, there are times when we can't do it alone. Recognizing when that is and who to seek help from is crucial for our lifelong success and wellbeing.

End of Module 3 – Reflection on Control

This reflection guides us in pursuing a change that will positively impact our lives. As we work on self-improvement, one of the most important lessons is to distinguish between what we can control and what we can influence, and to accept what lies beyond both.

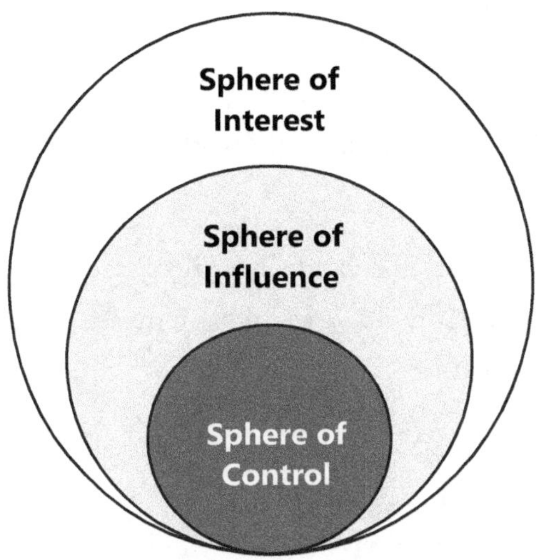

Figure 3.2 The Spheres of Interest, Influence, and Control

Use the prompts below to help direct your energy to where it matters most.

Step 1. Prioritize Your Change

Think of a specific challenge you're facing now, like high work stress, unhealthy eating, or ongoing poor sleep. Then, pick one small, safe, meaningful, and simple change you need or want to make—something that feels both important and within reach right now.

- The specific change I want to make is:
- Why this matters to me and how it relates to my values and well-being is:

Step 2. What Can You Control?

Considering your prioritized change, which parts are entirely within your control? Reflect on your decisions, efforts, focus, and how you manage your own thoughts and feelings.

- The aspects of this situation I can fully control are:
- The personal strengths, habits, or skills I can use or enhance to support this change are:

Step 3. What Can You Influence?

Some things you can't control, but you can influence them by shaping your environment as much as possible.

- The people, systems, or environments I can realistically influence to help implement this change include:
- Ways I might communicate or collaborate to enhance this influence are:

Step 4. What's Beyond Both?

Regarding your change, many factors are beyond your control and influence. Recognizing this helps you avoid unnecessary struggles.

- Regarding the change I am working towards, things outside my control or influence that I can let go of are:
- I can remind myself to let go or be compassionate with myself when these come up by:

Step 5. Action Shift

Focus your energy on what matters most.

- A small, specific, and meaningful step I will take today that I can control is:
- One supportive action I will undertake within my sphere of influence is:
- One way I'll recognize I'm making progress, even if it's small, is:

Quick Compass Reset: When you feel overwhelmed, pause and ask yourself: Is this within my control, my influence, or beyond both? Refocusing this way frees your energy to concentrate on the change that matters and is achievable.

Next Up

The Past, Present, and Future.

Module 4: Cultivate A Change Mindset

Swim with the current of life rather than against it, and swim to the best of your ability.

Learning Objectives. By the end of this module, you will be able to:

1. Examine how constant change affects your life and develop strategies to accept it rather than oppose it.
2. Reflect on lessons from your past and show how to let go of patterns or beliefs that no longer benefit you.
3. Practice present-moment awareness to clearly differentiate between what is and what could be your future.
4. Understand that lasting change doesn't come from adding more or waiting for the perfect time, but from intentionally using what you have now to make effective, sustainable progress.

What Is It?

A change mindset empowers us to let go of the past, which is unchangeable, and embrace the present as we look toward the future. By accepting where we are, in this time and place, without judgment or harsh self-criticism, we free ourselves to pursue meaningful change.

By cultivating a change mindset, we acknowledge that everything around us is in constant flux. Adopting a flexible and proactive approach to self-improvement helps us face new challenges and opportunities. It involves learning from the past without holding on to it, while staying engaged in the present to build a better future.

Successful self-improvement is always achievable with the right mindset. A change mindset has three connected parts—What Was, What Is, and What Will Be—each of which we'll examine in the following pages.

To cultivate a change mindset, we:

Let Go of What Was
Accept and Embrace What Is
Pursue What Will Be

Why It Matters

Personal growth stems from how we handle change. Sometimes life pushes us past our comfort zone, requiring us to adapt. Other times, we're attracted to unexpected opportunities. Either way, the decisions we make in response shape who we become.

When we intentionally embrace change, we build the strength to face challenges head-on and the courage to seek new opportunities. Instead of drifting aimlessly, we begin to guide our own path. We stop being passive spectators in life and start taking responsibility for our self-improvement.

More than just flexibility, a change mindset involves fully engaging with the present. It means aligning our goals with who we are and who we want to become. With this mindset, setbacks become lessons, uncertainty becomes possibility, and discomfort signals growth.

That's why it matters: by adopting a change mindset, we turn life from something that just happens to us into something we actively shape. It enables us to learn and grow consistently toward our highest potential—in our careers, relationships, and lifelong pursuits.

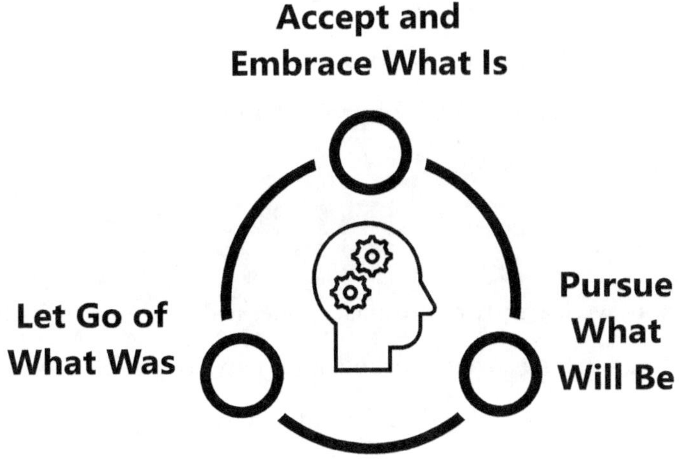

Figure 4.1 Cultivate a Change Mindset

Part 1: Let Go of What Was

Recall an experience that was either particularly good or the absolute worst.

When you've experienced something great, you might have thought, Wow, this is the best! I hope it never ends! Or when you've gone through something terrible, you may have asked yourself, When will this misery end?

Whether the experience was exceptionally good, the worst ever, or anywhere in between, it's now "What Was."

The past cannot be changed. Whether it was good or bad, it's now behind us. While we cannot alter the past, we reflect on it without judgment to learn from our experiences. And then, we let it go. Without dwelling on What Was, we use relevant lessons learned to plan changes that can measurably improve our lives.

Letting go of the past is crucial for grounding us in the present as we prepare to improve our future.

Practical Application

Through reflection, we learn from our past successes and failures. This practice involves analyzing what worked and why, as well as what didn't work and the reasons behind those outcomes.

Imagine we completed a complex project at school or work that required specific skills relevant to a change we are now considering. How did we leverage our strengths to achieve this? What feedback did we receive from others that confirmed our success? Is what we did repeatable today, given our current circumstances, to accomplish the change we need or want?

Basically, what did success look like, and what past experiences can we use to achieve self-improvement now?

On the other hand, consider a situation where we didn't meet our goals but are thinking about trying a similar change again. Did we fall short because of a lack of skills or abilities? Did we face a major life event or other challenges that were too big to overcome? Did we run out of time or money? Without judging, what lessons did we learn from this experience that can help us approach things differently this time?

Reflecting on our past experiences, we use what we've learned to embrace change while releasing What Was—whether good or bad—to focus on What Is.

Challenges and Pitfalls

One of the hardest parts of our change journey might be letting go of What Was. This process can be complex, and while reflection and personal effort are vital, there may be times when we realize that we can't navigate this path alone. It's important to recognize when persistent thoughts about our past become overwhelming.

If we find ourselves in this situation, seeking help from professionals can support our healing and help us move forward. Remember, transformation often begins when we face our deepest wounds, allowing us to embrace the possibility of a brighter future, free from the shadows of our past. Every step we take toward healing is a step away from our former selves and an important move toward reclaiming our lives and making meaningful changes.

Timeless Wisdom

This idea about the temporary nature of everything has been around since the beginning of human history. We return to timeless advice that provides useful insights into our daily lives.

There's a story in both Sufi and Jewish traditions about an ancient king who asked his wise men to craft a phrase that would bring him back to reality, whether he felt joyful or sad. They gave him the saying: "This, too, shall pass." The king was deeply moved by this saying and had it inscribed on a ring to always remind him.[41]

The phrase was popularized in the United States by figures like Abraham Lincoln, who, for example, referenced it in an address before the Wisconsin State Agricultural Society in 1859.[42]

"This, too, shall pass" reminds us that, as good as something is right now, it won't last. On the other hand, this saying offers a new perspective that helps build our resilience during times of despair. We find comfort in knowing that no matter how bad a situation may be at the moment, it won't last forever. Nothing does.

Whether it's as good as it can get, as bad as it can get, or anything in between, and no matter what it is, it will become What Was.

Another lesson for adapting to inevitable change comes from the Buddha, who is believed to have lived between the sixth and fourth centuries BCE. Central to his teachings are the concepts of impermanence (*anicca*) and suffering (*dukkha*).

Anicca teaches us that everything in life—our circumstances, thoughts, and perceptions—is constantly changing. Nothing remains the same. Dukkha teaches us that as things fade away, we suffer when we resist this natural flow by clinging to what we desire or hope will last forever.

To avoid this suffering, we accept the impermanence of all things and let go when the time comes. And inevitably, that time will come for things we cherish. However, this act of letting go is not about resignation or passivity; it is about accepting the truth that change is unavoidable and essential for growth.

As we learn from *The Teaching of Buddha*, recognizing and accepting that everything eventually ends can be unsettling, but it also encourages us to shift our perspective. That is, progress, continuous growth, and reproduction are also signs of endless renewal.[43]

Change isn't just about losing something; it also provides an opportunity for ongoing growth and renewal. When we let go of what has naturally come to an end, we allow ourselves to pursue new opportunities, growth, and transformation.

Change shouldn't be feared but embraced—a positive force that fosters personal development and the unfolding of our lives. Ultimately, releasing the past allows us to accept the present and actively work toward a better future.

Instead of holding onto What Was, we accept What Is and work toward What Will Be.

By seeing change as both an ending and a new beginning, we align ourselves with life's constant flow, helping us grow, improve, and find meaning in the impermanence that once felt intimidating.

Part 2: Accept and Embrace What Is

By practicing self-compassion in the present moment, we direct our focus and energy to the here and now.

The Unchangeable: Importantly, we differentiate between what is unchangeable—the past and some present circumstances—and what we can change. We then focus on self-improvement accordingly.

The common phrase "It is what it is" reminds us to accept present realities beyond our control or influence. When facing an unwanted situation, instead of resisting or dwelling on it, we acknowledge it and adapt accordingly.

This acceptance frees us from pointless efforts to change what we can't, lowering stress and frustration and allowing us to focus fully on what we can improve in our lives.

The Changeable: When something is within our control or influence to improve, and we are prepared, willing, and capable of acting, our self-help efforts become deliberate and meaningful.

We make intentional, measurable changes that align with our current capabilities and resources. Importantly, we pursue these changes with the minimum effort needed, ensuring progress and sustainability while preventing burnout. As we've seen earlier, for self-improvement, we avoid forcing change or pursuing it for its own sake. Maybe we're satisfied and have no reason to change right now, or we have a need or desire to change, and we plan accordingly.

Practical Application

With planned personal change, we avoid impulsive, radical shifts. We take deliberate steps toward our goals, informed by self-awareness and guided by self-mastery. This method allows us to recognize the right moments and ways to act without forcing progress, which can cause extra stress.

Crucially, accepting and embracing What Is does not imply complacency.

It involves recognizing what is within and beyond our control and influence, then focusing on improving ourselves based on our current circumstances. By aligning our efforts with life's natural flow, we reduce frustration and direct our energy toward achievable change.

Accepting and embracing What Is allows us to maintain a balanced approach to life, continually seek self-improvement, avoid unnecessary struggle, respect the limits of our control and influence, and intentionally pursue meaningful, achievable goals.

Challenges and Pitfalls

Accepting and embracing What Is can be difficult, especially when it forces us to face challenges we didn't choose. At times, this discomfort makes it harder to envision or pursue What Will Be.

Acceptance is not resignation; it's the starting point for meaningful change. By honestly assessing our strengths, weaknesses, and current situation, and remaining open-minded, we can identify where our efforts will have the greatest impact. This allows us to focus our energy on what we can directly control or influence, rather than wasting effort on what cannot be changed.

Self-awareness involves recognizing the parts of our current reality that can't be changed and moving forward. When we focus too much on these aspects—replaying them, resisting them, or blaming ourselves or others—we often feel frustrated and stuck. Accepting what cannot be changed is not giving up; it's choosing to stop fighting reality so we can act more effectively within it.

A clear sign that we might be reaching our limits is when effort no longer yields progress, clarity, or learning, but instead causes repeated distress, self-criticism, or paralysis. In today's world, seeking help is not a sign of failure or a lack of self-reliance; rather, it is a wise choice. Support from trusted friends, family members, colleagues, professionals, or new perspectives can broaden our options and help us regain momentum as we move forward.

Balancing what we can do for ourselves, given who and where we are right now, with a willingness to seek help when needed, fosters sustainable growth. This balance builds resilience, enhances self-understanding, and makes space for meaningful, lasting change.

If an effort consistently improves clarity, agency, or skill, it's probably worth continuing. If it consistently causes distress without progress, it might be time to seek support.

Timeless Wisdom

For historical context, we again look to ancient Greek philosophy, specifically Stoicism. This philosophy encourages us to acknowledge the reality of a situation, even if it is unpleasant or unfavorable, and to avoid dwelling on its negativity. Instead, as we saw in Module 3: Focus on Control, we direct our thoughts, choices, and actions toward improving what is within our power to change.

And we revisit Chinese philosophy to explore the timeless principle of *wu-wei* (pronounced in English as woo-way), often translated as "non-action" or "effortless action." Wu-wei offers valuable insight into accepting and embracing What Is and pursuing goals without trying to force outcomes.[44]

As Lao Tzu said:[45]

> The softest thing in the world dashes against and
> overcomes the hardest; that which has no
> substantial existence enters where there is no
> crevice.
>
> I know hereby what advantage belongs to doing
> nothing with a purpose.
>
> There are few in the world who attain to the
> teaching without words, and the advantage
> arising from non-action.

This passage emphasizes the importance of embracing What Is by highlighting life's natural flow and the effectiveness of non-resistance. It clarifies that acceptance is not complacency, but a graceful adjustment to circumstances beyond one's control.

Wu-wei encourages minimal effort in the face of challenges, suggesting that gentle actions can often be more effective than force. By aligning ourselves with the natural flow of life, we can accept things as they are, leading to a more peaceful existence without unnecessary struggle. In doing so, we develop resilience and adaptability, responding to life's ups and downs with ease and wisdom.

In short, as we accept and embrace What Is, we swim with the flow of life rather than against it and swim to the best of our ability.

Part 3: Pursue What Will Be

We're born to face challenges, adapt, and grow. We're naturally wired to learn, develop, and thrive. It's in our very nature to seek something more, something better in our lives. No matter where we start from, in this moment and place, there's always room to grow and improve.

To accomplish this, we take action.

We take meaningful self-improvement action that helps us move toward what we need and want while staying true to our core values. Although the desire for growth is universal, each person's path to success is uniquely personal. As we've seen, our self-improvement efforts are tailored to our individual situations: to each their own.

In the United States, many of us have probably seen or heard the Army's recruiting slogan, "Be All You Can Be." This phrase encourages aiming for something bigger and better. While it primarily serves as a recruiting message targeting young adults, it also reminds everyone to reach their full potential, regardless of age. It's a call for self-improvement, self-discovery, and making the most of our talents.

While broad ideals like these can inspire us to reach our potential, it's crucial to remember that fulfillment comes from achieving meaningful goals. Who we are and where we stand together help us set realistic goals for where we need or want to be.

Focusing on what matters most to us, rather than on what others consider success, brings fulfillment. No matter our circumstances, we are motivated to pursue what is truly important. Even the smallest deliberate step can break the cycle of stagnation, and small victories can increase motivation to keep growing.

Practical Application

Self-improvement occurs when we align our efforts with our values, even if the first steps are small. When we take action—no matter how little progress we make—we build momentum that encourages further growth.

The journey toward self-improvement isn't always easy. We'll face internal challenges, such as fear of failure, doubt, or procrastination. Recognizing these obstacles as natural parts of the process allows us to approach them with compassion and resilience.

We take deliberate action toward our goals by overcoming fears and procrastination rather than letting these challenges control us. Each step forward increases our sense of ability, helping us build the confidence to pursue what we need or want.

Our journey is uniquely ours. We embrace our natural desire to grow, pursue what matters to us, and take time to reflect on our progress. With each step, we move closer to a fulfilling and meaningful life that aligns with who we want to become.

Change often seems simple on paper: past, present, future. But it can be complex. No two situations are identical, which is why a one-size-fits-all self-improvement plan rarely works.

Challenges and Pitfalls

Sustainable progress can be achieved by designing a change plan tailored to your lifestyle, addressing your unique challenges, and aligning with your personal goals and values. Additionally, it is important to make necessary adjustments along the way to stay on track with your journey of change.

One of the biggest hurdles in self-improvement is managing life's dynamics. Life happens—unexpected events, changing feelings, and competing demands constantly challenge our resolve. In addition to external pressures, we face internal resistance to leaving our comfort zones. Old habits pull us back, and fears of failure or judgment hold us back from progress.

To make matters even more difficult, we often set unrealistic expectations, believing that significant change will happen overnight, when growth often happens slowly and irregularly. These challenges often cause common mistakes.

Sometimes, we overplan and underact—spending too much time and effort on designing the perfect strategy and never taking the first step. Other times, we sabotage ourselves by comparing our progress to someone else's, forgetting that every journey is unique. When we overlook small wins along the way, change feels distant and even impossible, making it too easy to give up.

The good news is that each obstacle can be overcome. Keep things simple, clear, and achievable. Don't wait for the perfect plan— take the next step, no matter how small. Build self-mastery by understanding your triggers, values, and habits, and adapt your strategy to your reality instead of copying someone else's plan.

And above all, remain dedicated to purposeful action, which is another lasting idea we will examine in the next module.

Timeless Wisdom

Over a lifetime, what drives us to pursue What Will Be? For perspective, history provides valuable insights into life's meaning. In this section, we introduce three enduring, overarching ideas about taking deliberate action.

First, having a purpose, which we'll explore in more detail in Module 5. Looking ahead, one concept, *ikigai* (pronounced EE-key-guy), from Japan, dates back at least 1,000 years and means "that which makes life worth living." More than just a grand life purpose, ikigai often resides in small daily joys that give life direction and meaning. Some modern self-help advice, like "finding your why," echoes this ancient wisdom, reminding us that what feels modern often has deep roots in human history.

Second, living with integrity. Going back to ancient Rome, in *Meditations*, Marcus Aurelius said:[46]

> No longer talk at all about the kind of man that a
> good man ought to be, but be such.

Here, he emphasizes the importance of taking action rather than getting caught up in endless debate. He argues that our true character is revealed in what we do, not in what we say. In the broader context of *Meditations*, he advocates for personal integrity and living in harmony with our words and actions. This serves as a powerful reminder not to overthink ourselves into analysis paralysis, but to take actionable steps toward becoming the person we aspire to be.

Third, take that step forward. We return to Lao Tzu, who is often associated with the saying: "A journey of a thousand miles begins with a single step." In the *Tao Te Ching*, we learn:[47]

> The tree which fills the arms grew from the
> tiniest sprout; the tower of nine stories rose from
> a small heap of earth; the journey of a thousand li
> commenced with a single step.

Lao Tzu highlights the importance of taking action, no matter how small, even on the longest and most challenging journeys. Progress often comes slowly, but acting is crucial for reaching our ultimate goals.

No matter how daunting a task may seem, it becomes less overwhelming once we decide to begin.

Our three-phase training program concentrates on the *how*—how you can help yourself change. It's designed to build skills and develop a strategy to achieve and maintain planned personal change, tailored to your unique circumstances.

No matter your background or starting point, this "how" is effective.

Along the way, you may find that your how guides you closer to your *why*—or that your *why* becomes clearer as you take action. Even if your purpose feels uncertain, deliberate growth has a way of sharpening your motivation and revealing what matters most.

For more ideas on uncovering meaning, see Module 5: Find Your Purpose, where we explore concepts that connect your personal *how* to your deeper *why*.

Anecdote: The DoD Change Machine

A Systems Lesson on How Big and Small Changes Really Work

Initially, I didn't learn to manage change through books, seminars, or motivational speeches. I learned it within an organization that views continuous change as essential for survival and plans accordingly.

In the Army—and more broadly within the Department of Defense—change is not seen as a disruption. It's regarded as inevitable. Missions change. Threats arise. Technologies progress. Entire domains of warfare come and go within a single generation, or even faster. Standing still isn't an option.

What impressed me most wasn't just the size of the organization or the importance of its mission. It was how systematic and emotionless the department was about managing change. There was no drama in letting go. No guilt about upgrading or shifting. Aside from a few select relics kept for a museum or static display at the main gate of a base, there was little nostalgia for things that had already fulfilled their purpose.

Change wasn't motivational. It was structural.

Over time, I began to see the DoD not just as an institution, but as a massive change machine—a system intentionally designed to let go of What Was, accept and embrace What Is, and continually pursue What Will Be, ever growing without collapsing under its own weight.

And that mindset—more than any tactic or technique—is what many of us lack when we try to improve our lives.

Change as a Managed System, Not an Emotion

Few organizations on earth are driven by the pursuit of constant change quite like the Department of Defense. Its mission—*to provide the military forces needed to deter war and ensure our nation's security*—requires continuous adaptation. The department doesn't wait for certainty; it plans amid uncertainty as a routine practice.

But here's the main point that is often missed: The DoD doesn't rely on motivation, inspiration, or willpower to change. Instead, it depends on structure, funding, and clear processes. Change occurs because resources are intentionally allocated for it—and because the system ensures what needs to be protected is secured first.

At the highest level, the department's budget reflects this mindset. While the numbers are enormous, the categories themselves are what matter. The DoD separates its resources into distinct functions, each serving a different role in the continuous cycle of transformation:

- Operations and Maintenance (O&M). This is specific funding to sustain the day-to-day readiness of the force, including civilian pay, training, equipment repairs, fuel, healthcare, information technology, and base operations support.
- Procurement: This funding is to buy military equipment—new or replacement—including vehicles, weapons, munitions, communications systems, and other hardware needed to equip the force. It covers the cost of acquiring these systems once they are developed and ready for initial fielding or replacement in support of What Is.
- Research, Development, Test, and Evaluation (RDT&E): Here, funding is provided for What Will Be to discover, develop, and test future military capabilities before they are ready for procurement and deployment.

These aren't abstract accounting categories. They embody a three-pronged approach: Prioritize sustainability. Equip and replace intentionally. Experiment purposefully.

And, crucially, when something no longer supports the mission, the department doesn't cling to it. It disposes of it.

What Was – Letting Go and Moving On

Military museums remind us that even the most advanced capabilities eventually become outdated. Radios, uniforms, weapons, vehicles, vessels, and aircraft—each one tells a story of development, operational importance, service, and eventual replacement.

While museums display the distant past, we can observe What Was in real time by visiting a Defense Logistics Agency Disposition Services site. There, we see an enormous inventory of turned-in equipment—much of it still fully functional. Aviation gear, laptops, servers, tools, medical equipment, uniforms, and countless other items sit waiting for their next destination. These items aren't necessarily discarded because they're broken; many are returned simply because the department has upgraded, replaced, or no longer needs them. In fast-moving areas like information technology, this turnover happens predictably. What we see here has reached the end of its scheduled usefulness or has become excess, and units turn it in accordingly.

Whether it is serviceable or not, if it has been turned in at a disposition site, the unit no longer needs or wants to keep it. Turning it in removes it from their property book, saving time, effort, and money for other, more important tasks.

That's the part that stayed with me.

The moment something is relinquished, it becomes What Was, and it no longer costs the organization anything.

Our lives often contain inventory equivalents: old commitments, unused subscriptions and memberships, unfinished projects, and purchases tied to identities we no longer embody. None of these are necessarily bad. They are simply no longer relevant to the mission we're on now.

The difference between us and the department is that we might still be paying for What Was long after it had lost its usefulness. We pay with money, attention, energy, and maybe guilt and underlying stress. Often, we're still paying because we borrowed to get it in the first place.

Beware the Debt Trap

A key difference between the Department of Defense and many of us is that the department doesn't depend on borrowed money to do what it needs or wants to do. It is fully funded upfront to sustain itself and acquire what it needs for What Is, all while earnestly working toward What Will Be.

Most of us work with limited resources: time, energy, attention, and money. When we use debt to make changes, we face a potentially risky disconnect of motivations.

The motivation to acquire something is usually optimistic:

- This will make my life easier.
- This will help me become who I want to be.
- This will solve the problem.

But the motivation to repay that same thing is often entirely different:

- Obligation
- Scarcity
- Pressure
- Stress

These motivations don't reinforce each other—they collide.

That collision is the debt trap.

Unlike the DoD, which can promptly dispose of what it no longer wants to sustain, we often can't—because we're still paying for it. We're stuck sustaining What Was at the expense of What Is and What Will Be.

This isn't a moral failing. It's a systems problem.

What Is – Sustaining Readiness

One of the largest parts of the DoD budget is Operations and Maintenance (O&M). O&M funds the department's essential needs—the costs of staying prepared today. It includes training, repairs, fuel, base operations, medical support, utilities, information technology, and the salaries for its civilian staff.

In short, O&M funds the day-to-day activities that sustain military readiness.

Notably, while the department pursues new capabilities or bold transformations, it also ensures that the force it has today can operate, adapt, and respond immediately.

Each of us has a personal O&M account. Readiness—our ability to function, cope, and respond—depends on it. Nutrition, sleep, shelter, safety, stability: these are our sustainment lines. When they're underfunded, our entire life becomes brittle.

A good place to start any change journey is with an honest, accurate self-assessment of your What Is. How much time, effort, and money does it take to sustain your current lifestyle? Are all your basic needs reliably met? Do you have any margin—financial, physical, or mental?

If the answer is yes, you might have the capacity to pursue What Will Be without becoming overwhelmed, financially strained, or regretful. If the answer is no, then—without judgment or harsh self-criticism—your current work may simply be to stabilize What Is. That is, to fully fund your personal O&M account before taking on more. Where we are might not be where we need or want to be, but for self-improvement, it is where we're starting from, and that matters.

Ironically, people with very little are sometimes better positioned to change than those burdened by debt and despair. When you start with nothing, you can grow intentionally at a pace you can sustain. When you're carrying more than you can afford, every step forward feels heavier than it should—and that's often a sign to lighten the load.

The takeaway for all of us, no matter where we begin: readiness comes first. With everything else going on in life, sustain your wellbeing. Fund your O&M account.

What Will Be – Investing in Change

In the DoD, Research, Development, Test, and Evaluation (RDT&E) represents its pursuit of What Will Be. Here, ideas are tested, prototypes are built, and new capabilities are explored. Some efforts fail. Many never scale. That's expected.

But RDT&E isn't funded by skipping meals, losing sleep, or deferring maintenance. The department doesn't sacrifice its readiness for ambition.

That's where our approach to change often goes wrong.

Many of us don't have separate budgets for sustainment, procurement, and transformation. We fund everything from the same limited pool. That means we must be intentional.

The most dependable starting point for personal change is also the simplest: begin with what you already have.

Modern self-help culture often suggests the opposite—that the right purchase, program, or product will unlock motivation and consistency. Fitness is a classic example. We buy memberships, apps, wearables, equipment, supplements, and gear, believing each one is the missing piece.

But sustainable progress often requires much less.

Sometimes all you need is the clothes you already own, fifteen minutes of free time, and a walk.

That may sound small, but it's not. It's practical, effective, and—most importantly—repeatable.

Sustainable change doesn't, and can't, come from endlessly adding resources. It comes from working within constraints and reallocating existing resources.

Of course, the department operates on a scale that none of us will ever match. It has unique, fully funded, debt-free budgets for sustainment, procurement, and transformation. It can support and acquire what it needs for What Is all while pursuing transformative, globally impactful change—sometimes on a scale that reshapes entire industries or technologies. That's the nature of an institution built on abundance.

If you want to see examples of this massive change machine in action—from the birth of the electronic computer, GPS, and the Internet to how a local unit expanded from just a couple of loaner cell phones into a structured mobile communications program—see the Appendix: DoD's Abundance. It shows what scaling up large and adding small look like, and why both are important.

Our Reality for Pursuing Change

Unlike massive institutions, we don't get infinite funding or endless second chances. Our lives operate under constraints. But constraints aren't obstacles—they're design parameters. A change mindset grounded in reality accepts the following:

- Stabilize before you pursue more. Growth happens from a strong foundation. Fund your personal O&M account first.

- Take a pay-as-you-go approach. Live within your means. Better yet, live below them. Capacity in reserve increases resilience.

- If you're tapped out, reduce before you add. Letting go of What Was frees resources to sustain What Is and pursue What Will Be.

- Design for bad days. Actions that require ideal conditions are fragile. Sustainable behaviors work on your worst ordinary day.

- Evaluate relentlessly. Movement without direction feels productive but produces nothing. Ask regularly: Is this supporting my mission?

Even small changes matter. For example, unsubscribing from irrelevant email lists, canceling unused memberships, or shutting down the laptop or putting down the phone to reclaim those fifteen minutes for a walk. That is, redirecting attention from something that does nothing for you to something that does, no matter how small it seems.

At first, it's less about outcomes and more about learning *how* to change—informed by self-awareness and guided by self-mastery, intentionally moving resources from low to high value. Like any skill, it becomes easier with practice.

The Change Mindset

The DoD exemplifies a highly refined and well-turned change machine: constantly evolving since 14 June 1775, the Army's birthdate, the largest and oldest branch. It faces What Was without regret, sustains What Is with discipline, and invests in What Will Be intentionally.

We don't have its resources. But we can adopt its change mindset.

This isn't a quick fix. This isn't wishful thinking. This isn't some obscure organizational theory. It's a systems approach to self-management—one that prioritizes our wellbeing and readiness, respects constraints, and views change as a skill rather than a feeling.

Let go of what drains you. Preserve what sustains you. Invest wisely in what's ahead. That's how complex systems survive. And that's how we can flourish as well.

Anecdote: A Small Cog in the Big Change Machine

Much self-improvement advice often assumes we have a luxury that many of us lack: the ability to obtain more. More time, more energy, more money, and more tools, systems, and support. When progress stalls, the common solution is to add more—buy this product, implement that strategy, or stack another routine. Failure to improve is often attributed to a lack of resources rather than to a problem with our approach. However, this line of reasoning applies to very few situations.

It works for large institutions because they can often afford to fix their problems. I spent two careers in one of the rare organizations—the Department of Defense—where adding resources is not only feasible but expected. When complexity overwhelms the system, additional personnel, increased funding, reorganization, or expanded authority are all valid responses.

Most of us don't have those options. And that difference matters.

The Army could meet new demands by adding resources, but I could not. My growth depended on working within fixed limits: time, energy, money, and rank. Instead of waiting to acquire more, progress came from making better use of what I already had. That required constantly reprioritizing—letting go of what no longer mattered and focusing on what did.

Starting from the Bottom, With a Long Way to the Top

I started adulthood as a teenage Army Private with almost nothing. I had no car, was living in the barracks, had no savings, earned the lowest pay on the pay scale, lacked workplace skills for a better job elsewhere, and had no family financial support.

What I did have—and was grateful for—was an opportunity, even if small, to build a good career. But that opportunity mattered only if I was willing to work my way up from the absolute bottom, with strict limits, while meeting all Army requirements to stay in.

Advancing in the Army required meeting increasingly high standards. I was in competitive specialties with limited opportunities for advancement, but staying in for a full career was governed by an "up or out" promotion system. Essentially, get promoted on time or be discharged. I soon realized that college credits, which counted as promotion points, played a significant role in promotion because many of the Soldiers I was competing against already had them.

The barrier to promotion and ongoing service wasn't a lack of motivation. It was my capacity.

This was before online education or anything online. Earning college credit required attending a class in person after a full duty day or on weekends. With long duty hours, deployments, constant training, and many extra duties assigned to a Private, I couldn't do everything I wanted to. So, I had to prioritize and do what I needed to do.

Most importantly, I needed to be promoted, which required earning sufficient college credits to remain competitive. That involved making choices.

Initially, I chose the most resource-efficient path available. I tested out of as many college classes as I could through the Defense Activity for Non-Traditional Education Support (DANTES) and the College-Level Examination Program (CLEP). What was required was studying on my own time, primarily using exam-preparation books and borrowing subject-matter books from the library.

When that wasn't enough, I began attending satellite college campus classes after duty hours and on weekends—often one or two per semester—wherever I was stationed, in the U.S. or abroad.

Every credit I earned replaced something else. My free time diminished, and other after-work activities dropped away. I accepted that trade because it was necessary for my career. Importantly, I kept a steady pace with my available time, effort, and money.

As an added benefit, studying for exams, taking tests, and setting aside time for an occasional class or two became a habit. That consistent habit mattered more than any single course.

Over the years, as I frequently moved between duty stations, I attended four different colleges. I also kept testing out of classes whenever I could. As my military training and experience grew, I earned additional college credits through the American Council on Education (ACE).

By the time I finally completed my undergraduate degree, it was assembled from seven different sources: four colleges, DANTES, CLEP, and ACE.

This isn't a path I recommend. Instead, it clearly shows how *not* to design an education plan from scratch. However, for many of us, this is what it looks like to work within real constraints—juggling a full-time job while trying to fit classes into our schedules to better our lives. In my case, I earned college credits as best I could, given my circumstances—without burning out.

The lesson is that we don't succeed by waiting for a perfect moment. It won't suddenly get easier next week, next month, or next year. Getting more before acting isn't an option. We move forward today by using what we already have with focus and purpose. Many others from all walks of life have advanced their careers this way—doing what they must with what they have, not what they wish they had, and doing so without feeling overwhelmed.

It's about self-awareness, prioritization, and progressing at a sustainable pace.

It took me more than ten years to finish an undergraduate degree. That timeline might make some people quit. It didn't make me quick, but it made me durable. Most importantly, I finished it, and that mattered way more than how long it took.

A Lesson About Managing Stress

Earning that first degree taught me an important lesson about self-improvement: growth demands stress, but lasting growth comes from stress you can recover from.

By staying within my time, emotional, and financial limits while managing the daily demands of Army life, I avoided burnout. Compared to a traditional college route, the pace was slow, but for me, it was sustainable.

And more: what started as a way to earn credits by testing out of college classes turned into a skill. Each test I took made the next one a little easier. Every small victory boosted my confidence. Over time, I became a highly effective test-taker not because I was naturally talented, but because I practiced with discipline.

It paid off. Earning that bachelor's degree jump-started my second career and enabled me to complete three additional graduate-level programs. Those credentials helped me reach the highest levels of the civil service—not because I moved faster, but because I kept going long enough to finish.

And that applies to everyone. Where you are right now doesn't have to be where you stay.

If you're competing with people who seem more educated, better resourced, or further along, it's normal to notice the gap. But the answer isn't to overwhelm yourself trying to close it all at once.

For many of us, self-improvement isn't limited by imagination; it's limited by reality. When we think that progress requires more hours, more effort, more money, and refuse to let go of something else, we can become exhausted, discouraged, surrounded by unfinished projects, in debt, and full of regret.

Progress doesn't come from endless accumulation. It results from alignment—choosing stress you can manage and recover from, maintaining effort that is sustainable, and setting goals that can withstand real life.

Live within your means. Better yet, live *below* your means. Consistent progress that aligns with your current life is more valuable than temporary gains that break it. Moving forward—at any speed—shapes what's possible.

Takeaways

- Let Go of What Was: It's history. We can't change what's unchangeable. Reflect on the past to learn from it without judgment or harsh criticism, and then move forward.

- Accept and Embrace What Is: Acknowledge your current situation and take a focused, balanced, and sustainable approach to changing what you can, considering who and where you are and where you need or want to be.

- Pursue What Will Be: Find a reasonable place between deficiency and excess. Set meaningful goals that meet your needs and fulfill your wants without overextending yourself, thereby avoiding burnout and regret.

- When starting your self-help journey, begin small—intentionally. The goal isn't to make a big change immediately; it's to learn *how* to change. Change is a skill, and like any skill, you'll improve with practice. Each small step increases self-awareness and builds self-mastery, confidence, and adaptability. As you practice managing smaller shifts, you'll find that bigger changes seem less intimidating—and much more within reach.

- Nothing too much: Growth involves releasing the past, being present, and moving toward the future. Sustainable progress depends on balance and sometimes asking for help. When we need help, we should seek it.

End of Module 4 – Readiness Survey

Self-directed change means learning from and letting go of the past, accepting and embracing who and where you are now, and moving toward what's next. It's not about forcing change; it's about aligning with growth. The following survey will help you explore your inner world with curiosity, honesty, and courage.

Change Readiness Survey: What Was, What Is, What Will Be

This survey can help you assess your readiness to manage change by reflecting on how you connect your past experiences, current reality, and future goals.

Note: This can be done as a standalone survey, but it is helpful to complete the previous self-assessments and module reflections in Phase One, from the Introduction through Module 3, first.

Section 1: What Was—Letting Go

> *Although we can't change the past, we don't forget it; instead, we learn from it. This is a key idea in knowledge management: our experiences are our most personalized teachers.*

Intent: Determine how previous experiences shape your views on personal growth.

Instructions: Rate each statement from 1 (Strongly Disagree) to 5 (Strongly Agree).

Let Go of What Was	**Rating (1–5)**
1. I can recall past changes I've experienced without feeling stuck in them.	
2. I actively reflect on lessons learned from previous successes and failures to apply to my current change.	
3. I can talk about past challenges without feeling defensive or regretful.	
4. I have identified patterns from my past that I do not want to repeat.	
5. I feel emotionally ready to release old habits, routines, or roles that no longer serve me.	

Reflection

- What lessons from the past are most helpful for the change I'm dealing with now?
- What do I still need to release to move forward?

Section 2: What Is—Accepting and Embracing the Present

Some aspects of the present are changeable, and some are not. Accepting who and where we are isn't approval—it's awareness. The more we dislike our current situation, the more motivated we should be to take action and make it better.

Intent: To evaluate how well you understand and accept your current reality as you consider a change.

Instructions: Rate each statement from 1 (Strongly Disagree) to 5 (Strongly Agree).

Accept and Embrace What Is	Rating (1–5)
1. I recognize my current level of stress, and if it's high, I will address it immediately.	
2. I have a clear understanding of my current strengths and weaknesses as I begin this change.	
3. I'm ready to learn new things about my change, and have suspended my preconceptions to do so.	
4. I'm aware of what I can control and/or influence about achieving my change, and accept those things I cannot.	
5. I accept who and where I am without judgment or harsh self-criticism, and without blaming others.	

Reflection

- What aspects of my current reality are within my control and influence as I pursue my change?
- Right now, what should I accept as my starting point for change?

Section 3: What Will Be—Visioning and Preparing for the Future

Sustainable change happens when we align our actions with what truly matters, choose goals that fit our reality, and take deliberate steps toward the future we want to live in.

NOTE: Planning for and implementing change requires motivation. A sign of this motivation is understanding that our future can differ from our present—and that we have the power to move toward something better. This section examines your readiness to pursue self-improvement at a high level. The goal here is to understand how open, motivated, and prepared you feel to take the first steps toward a better version of yourself.

As you progress through *Phase Two: Shape Your Environment* and then move into *Phase Three: Plan and Execute*, you'll set more detailed personal goals and develop effective strategies for change. For now, think of this survey as a baseline assessment of your readiness for change: a way to measure how honest you're willing to be, whether you accept that change might be necessary or desired, and how you begin preparing for that journey.

Intent: Evaluate your motivation, openness, and outlook on the future as you consider making meaningful personal changes.

Instructions: Rate each statement from 1 (Strongly Disagree) to 5 (Strongly Agree).

Pursue What Will Be	**Rating (1–5)**
1. I believe my actions can meaningfully improve my future.	
2. I'm willing to honestly examine my habits and routines to identify what may be limiting me.	
3. I'm ready to take small, imperfect steps forward, even without having the full plan.	
4. I'm willing to invest time and effort into my personal growth over the coming weeks and months.	
5. I'm willing to take small risks or try new approaches, even if I'm not certain they will work.	

Reflection

- What does a successful change look like compared to my current situation?
- What small steps will I take today toward gaining that experience?

Scoring and Interpretation

Add up your ratings for each section. Each section has a minimum score of 5 and a maximum of 25. The total score for the entire survey ranges from 15 to 75 points. There are no right or wrong answers— no good or bad scores. There isn't even an average score to compare with others.

Your score is just a snapshot of your current state. What matters is how you interpret its meaning and, more importantly, what you decide to do with that insight.

Only you hold the power to change yourself. Sometimes your results may indicate you're ready to move forward immediately. Other times, they may suggest that you should pause and address something unresolved before moving on. For example, if you find yourself held back by What Was or overwhelmed by What Is, it might be a sign to restore balance before pursuing What Will Be.

This survey, like every self-assessment in this book, is designed to help you help yourself. Use it as a mirror, not just a measure—a way to better understand your current state and identify where your energy, focus, and growth are most needed.

As your awareness grows, so does your ability to take intentional, effective action. That's the core of self-mastery—actions informed by honest reflection and a sense of purpose.

First things first: let's get our heads—and hearts—in this game. What does your score mean to you?

Next up

Considering what we've learned about the importance of self-awareness, setting aside our preconceptions, focusing on what we can control and strategically influence, and cultivating a change mindset, how does all of this impact our pursuit of transformation? We use our knowledge, narrow down our options, make rational decisions, and then take action to meet our needs and fulfill our wants in life.

A larger question, which might be the most important of all, could be: But *why?*

Module 5: Find Your Purpose

Throughout history, people from all walks of life have often asked a common question: What is the purpose of life?

Learning Objectives. By the end of this module, you will be able to:

1. Identify and prioritize your core values through a structured self-assessment, establishing a solid foundation for decision-making.
2. Let your values guide your daily choices and actions, providing direction for your growth even before your bigger purpose becomes clear.
3. Use your values to balance trade-offs and priorities, selecting options that best meet your needs now and align with your long-term goals.
4. Identify patterns in how your values appear across various situations, helping to develop deeper meaning and clarity of purpose naturally over time.

What Is It?

A Note on Terminology for This Module

Why We Use the Singular Word "Purpose"

People have always wondered why we exist and what gives life meaning. Philosophers call this telos or ultimate ends, while theologians refer to it as calling. Psychologists focus on motivation and self-actualization, while different spiritual traditions use terms such as *dharma*, destiny, or life path. In today's self-help talks, we often hear about "finding your why."

Each of these terms has its own history and nuance, shaped by the culture and worldview from which it originates. In this module, we use the word "purpose" as a common thread—not because it captures every nuance, but because it offers a clear, practical way to explore the deeper meaning of our choices, commitments, and growth. The language of purpose enables us to speak across the boundaries of philosophy, psychology, and religion, recognizing their vast diversity while sharing a common truth: the search for meaning, direction, and coherence is fundamental to the human experience.

Every culture has crafted its own answer, weaving purpose into daily life. The quest for it is a timeless theme, and each generation and tradition offers its own perspective—sometimes complementary, sometimes conflicting—but all converge on a shared truth: purpose is an essential part of the human experience.

For example, Aristotle discussed eudaimonia, a flourishing life guided by virtue and reason, as the highest goal of human existence. Centuries later, Alfred Adler defined purpose in psychological terms, suggesting that fulfillment comes not from isolated striving but from helping others succeed.

In contrast, Sigmund Freud emphasized the pursuit of pleasure and the avoidance of pain. At the same time, Carl Jung focused on individuation—the process of integrating the self—as the forces that give life its purpose. Viktor Frankl, who suffered as a prisoner in Nazi concentration camps and later founded logotherapy, a form of existential psychotherapy, showed that even in the bleakest conditions, life remains survivable when grounded in meaning.

Entire traditions have explored what gives human life purpose, coherence, and meaning. In Hindu thought, the concept of *dharma* represents a person's growing responsibilities within a moral and cosmic order—an orientation shaped by one's nature, stage of life, and community. In classical Chinese philosophy, purpose is often conveyed through harmony: the Confucian cultivation of virtuous relationships, the Daoist alignment with the natural flow of events, and ritual practices that connect human life with the larger cosmos.

Buddhism points toward liberation from suffering, teaching that a life rooted in compassion, mindfulness, and right action naturally becomes meaningful. Christianity combines a universal call—to love God and neighbor—with a sense of personal vocation, understood as the unique way one's gifts and circumstances serve that greater calling. In Japan, the modern concept of *ikigai* (reason for being) emphasizes the energy and satisfaction that come from where one's joys, talents, livelihood, and contributions to others intersect.

These perspectives do not offer a single answer, but together they show how deeply human the search for purpose is—and how many paths can guide a person toward a life that feels oriented and alive.

As this conversation has unfolded for millennia, welcome!

Now you're part of it!

Purpose shapes and guides our lives. It combines our desires, strengths, relationships, beliefs, and values into something greater—a life that feels meaningful and worthwhile. Without it, success might seem empty, and comfort can become restless.

What is my purpose? Throughout history, people have pondered this question:

- Philosophers discussed it in academies.
- Prophets and spiritual leaders described it as a calling or divine mission.
- Scientists and humanists examined it through reason and human potential.
- People in all cultures think about it during their quiet moments every day and everywhere.

In other words, if you've ever wrestled with questions about life's purpose, you're in good company.

At its core, purpose isn't a fixed, single answer but a way to guide your life. It involves what you do, as well as how you connect:

- To yourself through your gifts, passions, and values.
- To others through relationships, service, and contribution.
- To something greater—whether that's God, humanity, or the ongoing story of life itself.

And here's a liberating truth: purpose isn't necessarily fixed. It can evolve and shift as you do. What feels like purpose in your twenties might deepen in your thirties, forties, fifties, sixties, or seventies. Life circumstances change, and along with them, our sense of purpose may also evolve.

Seeking purpose is not about finding a single, definitive answer but about engaging in a lifelong conversation about *why* we do what we do. The power lies not in solving this question once and for all, but in living with greater clarity, intention, and authenticity throughout the journey.

Why it Matters

When life feels empty, confusing, or aimless, it's often because of a lack of purpose. While having purpose doesn't eliminate struggles, it changes how we confront them. Without purpose, challenges might seem pointless; with it, even suffering can become meaningful.

Purpose acts as our internal guide when the way ahead is unclear. While it may not give exact steps to reach our goals, it keeps us focused on what really matters.

People with a strong sense of purpose often experience greater resilience, hope, and overall wellbeing. Similarly, without it, spiritual traditions teach us that life can feel empty, no matter how much external comfort or success one has.

With purpose, our lives gain significance; our choices produce ripples, and we are part of a story larger than ourselves.

For those feeling lost, the importance of purpose is clear: it gives coherence to our lives, turning scattered days into a meaningful journey and inspiring us to get up each morning with something to aim for.

Practical Application

Purpose functions as an internal compass, guiding us toward what matters most. However, a compass alone doesn't propel us forward. To reach our destination, we need clear goals and specific steps that turn intention into ongoing action. While purpose provides motivation and meaning, goals establish structure, helping us measure progress and develop a sense of significance.

For example, if our sense of purpose is to teach others, the desire to empower them through knowledge explains *why* we do it. However, fulfilling this purpose requires a clear plan of *how* to achieve it. Teaching is a broad and diverse field that includes education, training, and experience. To teach effectively, we must be self-aware—deciding what we want to teach, recognizing our strengths, identifying areas for improvement, and developing specific plans to address those gaps.

Take MT, for example. She dreams of becoming a high school biology teacher who inspires young minds to explore the natural world. Her purpose guides her goals: she doesn't just want to teach facts about cells and ecosystems—she wants to spark curiosity and foster a deeper connection to life itself. To bring this purpose to life, she pursues a bachelor's degree in biology, completes a teacher preparation program, passes certification exams, and gains classroom experience. Each stage not only brings her closer to a fulfilling career but also to realizing her purpose.

Now consider AG, a freelance writer and entrepreneur who wants to teach storytelling and content creation through online courses. His aim is to help others find their voice and share their ideas with clarity and confidence. For him, writing isn't just a skill—it's a way to empower others to express what matters most. His goals of building a writing portfolio, designing instructional materials, and mastering learner-centered course design bring that vision to life. While formal credentials aren't strictly required, he still invests in courses on communication, marketing, and instructional design, continually refining his craft. By leveraging online platforms and social media, AG not only expands his audience but also harnesses his purpose to build a meaningful and sustainable livelihood.

Purpose ignites the spark—but it's clarity of method, disciplined goal-setting, and the courage to grow that turn that spark into lasting impact. Purpose gives us direction; goals drive momentum.

Challenges and Pitfalls

The pursuit of purpose can be both rewarding and challenging, and seekers often fall into familiar traps. Some become stuck in analysis paralysis—overthinking, overreading, overanalyzing, endlessly scrolling through online noise, and planning without ever taking action.

Others swing to the opposite extreme, jumping from one commitment to another and exhausting themselves before gaining real momentum. Another trap is expecting a quick fix and chasing trends and fads, mistaking popular advice or social validation for one's true direction.

Perhaps the most subtle yet damaging trap is living according to someone else's script—pursuing a career, lifestyle, or values that others expect rather than those that resonate within us. These challenges and pitfalls can leave us feeling unfulfilled, even if we seem successful on the surface.

This is where self-mastery becomes crucial. We define the process as follows: we are informed by self-awareness and guided by self-mastery. We use discernment to understand our inner state, assess our options, and then act—adapting our behavior as circumstances shift.

At its core, it's about the discipline of keeping our *how* aligned with our *why*.

It means recognizing when a fear of imperfection is holding us back. It involves pacing ourselves—focusing on a few meaningful, value-driven goals instead of spreading our energy across every opportunity that arises. It means pausing before jumping on the next trend to ask: Does this align with my core values, or is it just a distraction? And it means having the courage to stay true to our own convictions, even when they don't match the expectations of family, peers, or culture.

Self-awareness uncovers the truth. Self-mastery decides how to respond to it. Obstacles become opportunities to grow on our journey.

Each time we avoid analysis paralysis, overextension, or imitation, we build our ability to live more intentionally.

Over time, we realize that purpose is not a race to win or a mold to fit into, but a lifelong journey of taking intentional steps toward our goals and staying true to our inner compass.

Timeless Wisdom

When we ask, "What's my purpose in life?" we explore one of humanity's oldest debates. Throughout history and across civilizations worldwide, people have sought their purpose, leaving a wealth of wisdom to guide our own journey.

We have access to a vast, rich, and deep collection of recorded thoughts on the question of purpose in our exploration. Some of the greatest minds throughout history have wrestled with this very question, influenced by their eras, cultures, and personal struggles. Listening to their insights feels like walking through a hall of voices—each unique, yet all echoing the same longing for direction and fulfillment.

Their insights don't provide a single answer, but they can help us find new ways to understand our own. The following table presents a brief selection of thinkers and traditions on the purpose of life, organized in reverse-chronological order.[48]

Thinker / Tradition	Core Idea of Purpose	Key Emphasis
Maslow (1908–1970)	*Self-Actualization* — becoming what you are capable of being.	Purpose arises when higher needs are met and you express your true potential (creativity, authenticity, growth).
Frankl (1905–1997)	*Will to Meaning* — finding meaning even in suffering.	Purpose discovered through work, love, or attitude toward hardship.
Jung (1875–1961)	*Individuation* — kindling light in darkness.	Purpose is becoming whole: integrating self, expanding awareness, contributing to collective consciousness.
Adler (1870–1937)	*Belong / Contribute* — life means serving the whole.	Purpose is found in relationships, social belonging, and contribution to others.
Freud (1856–1939)	*Will to Pleasure* — seeking happiness through pleasure and avoiding pain.	Purpose is not cosmic but instinctual; pursuit of happiness is real but limited by reality and society.
Nietzsche (1844–1900)	*Will to Power* — self-overcoming and value creation.	Purpose is self-created by overcoming challenges, affirming life, and shaping one's own values.
Ikigai (Japan, 794 CE)	*Harmony and Balance* — reason for being in everyday life.	Purpose comes from integrating what you love, are good at, the world needs, and sustains you.
Aristole (384-322 BCE)	*Eudaimonia* — achieve a flourishing life of virtue and fulfillment.	Purpose is realized through cultivating moral and intellectual virtues in harmony with reason.
Spiritual Traditions (dating back thousands of years)	*Transcendence* — aligning with the sacred or ultimate reality.	Purpose is found through prayer, meditation, service, and transcendence of ego into faith, love, and compassion.

Table 5.1 Perspectives on Purpose

These, among many others, have helped shape the idea of purpose since the beginning of recorded history, which was influenced by oral tradition for countless generations before that.

Abraham Maslow (1908-1970)

A musician must make music, an artist must paint, a poet must write, if he is to be ultimately happy. What a man can be, he must be. This need we may call self-actualization.[49]

Maslow was an American psychologist best known for developing the hierarchy of needs. His humanistic psychology focused on growth, creativity, and the natural drive toward fulfillment, shaping modern ideas about purpose and wellbeing.

He proposed that we climb a ladder of needs—beginning with survival and safety, then love and esteem—until reaching the highest level: self-actualization. At this stage, purpose involves realizing what we are capable of becoming. Fulfillment comes not from living someone else's plan, but from expressing the deepest potential of our own nature.

Viktor Frankl (1905-1997)

Logotherapy focuses on the meaning of human existence as well as on man's search for such a meaning. According to logotherapy, this striving to find a meaning in one's life is the primary motivational force in man.[50]

Frankl was an Austrian neurologist, psychiatrist, and Holocaust survivor who founded logotherapy, an existential approach centered on the human pursuit of meaning. His book, *Man's Search for Meaning*, has inspired millions with its lessons on resilience, freedom, and purpose, even amid the harshest suffering.

In his book, Frankl compares his idea of purpose with those of two other major thinkers of his era. He differentiates his *will to meaning* from Sigmund Freud's *will to pleasure* and Alfred Adler's focus on the *will to power* (see Freud and Adler, below).

Life, Frankl argued, is only bearable when we find meaning in it—whether through bringing something to life, loving someone, or facing suffering with dignity. He reminds us that even in darkness, a sense of purpose can be the light that guides us.

Carl Jung (1875-1961)

As far as we can discern, the sole purpose of human existence is to kindle a light in the darkness of mere being.[51]

Jung was a Swiss psychiatrist who founded analytical psychology and introduced key concepts like archetypes, the collective unconscious, and individuation. His work connected psychology with philosophy, myth, and spirituality, greatly influencing modern ideas about the human search for meaning.

For Jung, purpose means becoming more whole—bringing together the conscious and the unconscious, the shadow and the light —until we are aligned with who we are at our core. While Sigmund Freud (see below) focused on instinct and survival, Jung pointed toward transcendence, imagination, and the sacred aspect of human life.

Alfred Adler (1870-1937)

Human beings live in the realm of meanings. We do not experience pure circumstances; we always experience circumstances in their significance for men. Even at its source our experience is qualified by our human purposes. Life means—to contribute to the whole.[52]

Adler was an Austrian doctor and psychotherapist who founded individual psychology, emphasizing the importance of social connection and personal goals in human growth. He also introduced the idea of the "inferiority complex."

Although different in temperament, Alder echoed Friedrich Nietzsche's theme of self-overcoming or *will to power* (see Friedrich Nietzsche below). He also believed that human beings are constantly striving, but for Adler, the measure of purpose was not dominance but contribution—that is, to belong, to serve, and to help others.

Sigmund Freud (1856-1939)

The question, "What is the purpose of human life?" has been asked times without number; it has never received a satisfactory answer; perhaps it does not admit of such an answer.[53]

Sigmund Freud, an Austrian neurologist and the founder of psychoanalysis, proposed influential ideas about the unconscious mind, including the id, ego, and superego, and how unconscious drives influence behavior.

Freud was skeptical that life had an inherent, higher purpose beyond religious belief. He argued that human behavior is primarily driven by the *pleasure principle*—the desire to seek pleasure and avoid pain. However, he also stressed that this drive cannot operate freely. The demands of reality—social norms, responsibility, and limitations—impose what he called the *reality principle.*

The reality principle reflects the ego's ability to delay gratification and to control the id's impulses in accordance with external reality. Instead of seeking immediate pleasure, we seek satisfaction in ways that are sustainable and socially acceptable, even if that means restraint or delay.

Freud concluded that this tension makes lasting happiness hard to attain—not because we desire the wrong things, but because the world cannot fully satisfy our desires.

In this way, he captures a familiar truth: we seek happiness, yet often find it to be partial, fragile, and just beyond reach.

Friedrich Nietzsche (1844-1900)

From the military school of life.—That which does not kill me, makes me stronger. (Maxims and Missiles, 8)

If a man knows the wherefore of his existence, then the manner of it can take care of itself. Man does not aspire to happiness; only the Englishman does that. (Maxims and Missiles, 12)[54]

Regarding the second quote above, Viktor Frankl recalls Nietzsche as saying: "He who has a *why* to live for can bear with almost any *how*."[55]

Friedrich Nietzsche was a German philosopher and cultural critic who challenged traditional morality, religion, and the idea of absolute truth. He stressed the importance of forming personal values, introduced the concept of the *will to power*, and proposed the ideal of the Übermensch (an overman, or higher man) who grows by mastering himself and overcoming adversity. Each challenge endured is a step toward becoming a fuller, stronger person. His ideas have greatly influenced modern discussions about meaning, purpose, and existential freedom.

Nietzsche believed that the purpose of life does not come from external sources; instead, it must originate from within ourselves. He argued that meaning is found through self-overcoming, which involves developing our own values and seeing life's challenges as opportunities for personal growth and strength.

Ikigai (Japan: originating in the Heian period, 794-1185 CE)[56]

Ikigai is a Japanese concept often translated as "reason for being," but it is more flexible than a Western idea of a single life purpose or vocation.

It suggests that fulfillment comes from combining everyday joys, responsibilities, and contributions, rather than pursuing a grand, abstract goal. Ikigai is less about a dramatic calling and more about a subtle balance: the things that give life meaning.

This can be as simple as tending a garden, caring for family, or practicing an art—activities that foster a sense of continuity and purpose.

Ikigai has recently become popular in the U.S. and is often depicted as the intersection of these four key aspects of life:[57]

What you love
What the world needs
What you can be paid for
What you are good at

When these elements come together, life feels meaningful because daily living shows coherence and balance, not because of external accomplishments. Unlike Freud's idea that human purpose depends on the tension between pleasure and pain, ikigai views purpose as coming from harmony: the small, steady practices that bring joy, usefulness, and stability.

In short, discovering one's reason for being is less about pursuing a final goal and more about cultivating rhythms of balance—in work, relationships, and practices that nourish both self and community. It is a dynamic process that constantly evolves as circumstances change, rather than a fixed endpoint.

Aristotle (384-322 BCE)

Aristotle explains that, just as "the function of a lyre-player is to play the lyre, and that of a good lyre-player is to do so well," so too the human being has a distinct purpose.

Thus, "human good turns out to be activity of soul in accordance with virtue," whose fullest expression is eudaimonia—not a passing feeling, but the flourishing that arises when a life is guided by reason and lived in virtue.

Importantly, eudaimonia requires the span of a complete life devoted to realizing this purpose. As Aristotle reminds us:[58]

For one swallow does not make a summer, nor does one day; and so too one day, or a short time, does not make a man blessed and happy.

Spiritual Traditions and Organized Religions

Beyond psychology and philosophy, entire traditions have developed around the question of purpose.

In humanity's ongoing quest for purpose, perhaps no voices have been more enduring and influential, and no thought deeper or broader, than those of the world's great spiritual traditions.

While the following summaries highlight common themes of purpose across traditions, they are not comprehensive and do not include all interpretations or schools of thought. The list is arranged in reverse-chronological order by founding date.[59]

Islam (7th century CE, Arabian Peninsula)

Many Islamic teachings emphasize living with devotion to Allah in every part of life (*ibadah*), practicing justice and kindness, serving as a moral steward (*khalifah*) of creation, and preparing for eternal life in the hereafter.

Christianity (1st century CE, Roman Judea)

A core theme in Christianity is to love God and one's neighbor, to follow the teachings and example of Jesus Christ, to live one's vocation through faith and service, and—according to many traditions—to seek salvation and transformation through divine grace.

Shinto (developed from prehistoric religious practices in Japan)

Purpose is to live in harmony with the *kami*—the spirits of nature, ancestors, and sacred places—through reverence, purity, and daily practices that maintain the balance among people, community, and the natural world.

Taoism (Daoism) (4th–3rd century BCE, China)

Taoist teachings focus on aligning with the Tao, the natural order of the universe, by embracing simplicity, inner harmony, spontaneity, and *wu-wei* (effortless action), allowing life to flow naturally.

Buddhism (6th–5th century BCE, India)

Buddhists teach that purpose is found in awakening from suffering (*dukkha*) by understanding the *Four Noble Truths*, practicing the *Eightfold Path*, cultivating compassion, and ultimately reaching liberation (*nirvana*) from the cycle of rebirth (or recurring suffering, depending on interpretation)—a journey that reminds us that growth and meaning come through ongoing practice and mindful change.

Confucianism (6th–5th century BCE, China)

Confucian thought stresses cultivating virtue—especially benevolence (*ren*) and proper conduct (*li*)—by fulfilling one's roles with integrity and contributing to a harmonious, ethical society through personal character and responsibility.

Judaism (emerging with Abraham c. 2000–1800 BCE; Torah codified later)

Jewish tradition emphasizes living in a covenant with God by following the commandments (*mitzvot*), acting with justice and mercy, sanctifying everyday life through ethical and ritual practices, and engaging in the repair and improvement of the world (*tikkun olam*).

Chinese Folk Traditions (prehistoric origins, evolving over millennia)

These traditions focus on honoring ancestors, maintaining harmony with cosmic forces like *qi* (vital life energy), and balancing *yin-yang* (the interconnected, complementary forces). They also involve preserving the connection between family, community, nature, and spirit—often in relation to Confucian and Taoist ideas.

Hinduism (origins 3000–1500 BCE)

Hindu teachings outline four goals of life (*purusharthas*): fulfilling moral duties (*dharma*), pursuing prosperity (*artha*), experiencing love and pleasure (*kama*), and ultimately achieving spiritual liberation (*moksha*). These goals collectively help guide a balanced and meaningful life.

Looking at some of the world's major religions and traditions, we see that life is meant for more than just serving ourselves. Whether through devotion to God, connection with nature, compassion for others, or caring for our communities, we are guided toward something larger, deeper, and more meaningful beyond self-centered living. Their diversity is a gift: it shows that purpose is not a single formula but a broad landscape of possibilities waiting to be explored.

At its core, life's purpose is to live in harmony with a greater reality—divine, cosmic, or natural—by cultivating virtue, caring for others, and following a path that leads to lasting fulfillment and wholeness.

As seekers of purpose, we aim to listen, reflect, and craft a life that is uniquely ours, rather than following someone else's path entirely.

In other words, to have our own purpose.

And that's something each of us has to discover on our own.

Anecdote: What's My Purpose?

As a teenager stepping into adulthood, I wasn't driven by a grand vision. I didn't wake up each day with a clear purpose—or even think much about it. My goals were simple and immediate: what to eat, where to sleep, and how to earn enough money to make it through another day. Life was about survival, not significance.

Over time, through experience, reflection, and a few tough lessons, I realized that purpose isn't something you suddenly find—it's something you nurture. It evolves. It's not a single moment of insight, but a gradual awakening shaped by choices, responsibilities, and values.

Our values—the beliefs about what matters to us and how we should live—guide us toward a sense of purpose. When we define what we stand for, we align our actions with a meaningful life. Purpose isn't just about reaching a specific goal; it's about consistently moving in a direction that reflects who we are.

As an active-duty Soldier, I operated under an up-or-out promotion system that required either advancement within a certain timeframe or a discharge. That environment made me question why I was pursuing self-improvement at all. However, I soon realized that self-improvement becomes meaningful when guided by values rather than anxiety, and is rooted in becoming rather than in deficiency. That difference—between growth driven by fear and growth driven by commitment—has stayed with me.

Earlier in my career, my motivation was simple: advance, achieve, succeed. I tracked progress through titles, promotions, and a steady climb upward. That drive worked well—until life expanded the perspective.

As I stepped into senior leadership, got married, and became a parent, something changed. Career success still mattered, but it was no longer the only thing. I started considering decisions not just by how they helped me professionally, but also by what they cost—or protected—at home. I found myself choosing presence over prestige more often, and surprisingly feeling at peace when I did.

Marriage and family have significantly reshaped my sense of purpose. My motivation now extends beyond personal achievement to include caring for others and building something lasting. Developmental psychologist Erik Erikson called this concept generativity—the adult drive to nurture, mentor, and give back beyond oneself. This drive is a crucial part of adult growth in the seventh stage of his psychosocial development theory.[60] Naming it helped me understand what I was already living.

As my purpose shifted, work became less focused on climbing higher and more about making meaningful, lasting contributions. I aimed to be a steady example for my family and to build a life defined not just by achievement but by security, stability, and contentment.

Career success didn't disappear—it found its place within a larger, more human purpose.

Over the years, as I transitioned from active-duty service in the Army to civilian life and eventually to my second retirement, my purpose has evolved. Family remains my top priority. In addition, I now dedicate myself to teaching, mentoring, and helping others discover their values and shape their futures. While the uniform may change, the mission stays the same: to serve, guide, grow, and teach others to help themselves.

As the saying goes, when you teach, you learn twice. While I have learned a lot over the decades, I am still learning.

It all comes down to evolving over a lifetime. Our values—such as career, family, security, wisdom, inner harmony, and a comfortable life—can coexist and change in importance as we go through life. And as Erikson showed, each stage of life presents a new question: early on, it might be Who am I?; later, What do I contribute?; and then, What endures after me?

Together, these questions show that purpose isn't a fixed goal but a changing conversation between our values and circumstances.

Purpose doesn't have to be grand or mysterious. It grows with you—through service, contribution, and steady, value-driven effort, one day at a time.

And maybe that's a helpful consideration: If you're unsure of your purpose, it won't suddenly appear by waiting around for it. Start living.

Whatever motivates you to make things better, for yourself and for a greater good, start doing it, and you'll find your purpose.

Honor what matters to you. Commit to lifelong growth. Be willing to serve something larger than yourself. Master yourself and practice change. And clarity will emerge.

Takeaways

- Purpose is both a universal and deeply personal journey, uncovered through unique experiences and beliefs.
- It involves connections with ourselves, others, and a wider context, enriching our lives and emphasizing contribution to something greater.
- The search for meaning is a continual process that demands deliberate effort and sincerity.
- Nothing too much. Having a purpose can be inspiring, but it's important not to obsess over finding one definitive answer. Embrace the journey of discovery and concentrate on continuous self-improvement that aligns with your values for a meaningful experience.

End of Module 5 – Values Survey

"Purpose" is as deeply personal as any philosophical or spiritual question can be, and discovering it is a journey only you can take.

No person or book—especially not this one—can decide your purpose for you. But when you're unsure about your purpose, take time to reflect on and assess your values.

Understanding your values is one of the most reliable ways to clarify your life direction. Purpose emerges from knowing what matters most and choosing to live in alignment with it.

This end-of-module survey helps you explore two essential dimensions of your values:

- End-state values—the life outcomes you ultimately aim for
- Behavioral values—the ways of being you want to embody as you work toward those outcomes

Ranking these values gives you a clearer sense of what you're aiming for and how you want to show up along the way.

Instructions: Ranking Your Values

1. Thoroughly review both of the lists below.

Read through all 15 end-state values and all 15 behavioral values before ranking anything. Let the words settle. Notice which ones feel familiar, energizing, or challenging.

2. Rank each list separately (1–15, with no ties).

For each list, 1 is the most important value to you, and 15 is still important but least central to your life right now.

Forced ranking matters. It works because values are evident only when trade-offs are necessary. If everything is important, then nothing is truly prioritized—and we risk getting stuck in analysis paralysis.

3. Rank based on aspiration, not performance.

Choose the values you *want to guide your decisions*, even if you don't always live up to them yet.

4. Expect tension and embrace it.

For instance, you may feel pulled between:

- Freedom and Security
- Love and Authenticity
- Courage and Patience
- Integrity and Kindness

These tensions are meaningful. They reveal the real choices you make when life gets complicated.

5. When finished, review your top five and bottom five from each list.

Your top values reveal your natural guiding principles. Your lower-ranked values are not bad values; they simply reflect what you are more willing to compromise when time, effort, and money are limited, which they often are.

Both sets offer insight into how you make choices under real-world constraints.

Academic Note: This exercise draws on decades of research in values psychology, beginning with the work of social psychologist Milton Rokeach in 1973. He distinguished between terminal (end-state) values—desired life outcomes—and instrumental (behavioral) values—preferred modes of conduct—and showed that people tend to organize these values hierarchically to guide decision-making.[61]

Building on Rokeach's work, social psychologist Shalom Schwartz developed a cross-culturally validated model of universal human values, showing how value priorities group into broader motivational areas that influence perception and behavior across cultures.

End-State Values (Desired Outcomes of Life)

What kind of life do I ultimately want to have lived?

RANK (1 - 15)	VALUE	SUMMARY OF VALUE
	Authenticity	Living in alignment with my true self
	Belonging	Being accepted and connected to others
	Contentment	Enduring wellbeing and life satisfaction
	Contribution	Having positively mattered to others
	Freedom	Autonomy and self-determination
	Fulfillment	A sense of completion and alignment
	Inner Peace	Emotional calm and acceptance
	Justice	Fairness and moral rightness in life
	Legacy	Leaving something of lasting value
	Love	Deep affection and care given and received
	Meaning	A life that feels significant and worthwhile
	Personal Growth	Becoming better over time
	Security	Safety, stability, and predictability
	Self-Respect	Dignity and pride in myself
	Wisdom	Deep understanding of life and self

Behavioral / Instrumental Values (Ways of Living)

How do I need to act consistently to reach what matters most?

RANK (1 - 15)	VALUE	SUMMARY OF VALUE
☐	Accountability	Willingness to be answerable
☐	Compassion	Caring about others' suffering
☐	Courage	Acting despite fear or discomfort
☐	Curiosity	Openness to learning and discovery
☐	Generosity	Giving time, energy, or resources
☐	Honesty	Truthfulness in word and action
☐	Humility	Realistic self-assessment and openness
☐	Integrity	Alignment between values and actions
☐	Kindness	Intentional goodwill toward others
☐	Mindfulness	Attentive awareness of the present moment
☐	Patience	Tolerance for delay and frustration
☐	Perseverance	Sustained effort over time
☐	Respect	Treating others with dignity
☐	Responsibility	Owning my choices and obligations
☐	Self-Discipline	Regulating impulses and effort

Reflection Questions: Integrating Your Values

These prompts help you connect the dots between what you want from life and how you behave as you pursue it.

1. Alignment: When examining your top end-state and behavioral values, what patterns surface about the kind of life you want and the person you aim to become?

2. Tension: Do any of your top end-state values conflict with your core behavioral values? What does this tension reveal about your inner state or your current life situation?

3. Support: Which one or two behavioral values, if practiced more consistently, would most speed up progress toward your highest-ranked end-state values? How might practicing them more intentionally alter your trajectory?

4. Blind Spots: Are there lower-ranked behavioral values that could still be crucial for achieving your desired end-state? What might be missed if they are overlooked?

5. Identity and Purpose: If someone watched your life for a month, which of your core values— from either list— would they easily notice in your actions? Which ones would you like them to see more of?

Module 6: Prove It to Yourself

The first principle is that you must not fool yourself—and you are the easiest person to fool. So you have to be very careful about that.—Richard Feynman[62]

Learning Objectives. By the end of this module, you will be able to:

1. Distinguish between considering ideas and taking action, and show how deliberate action produces tangible results.
2. Assess personal strategies and justify which approaches work best for your specific situation through self-guided research and reflection.
3. Recognize the risks of analysis paralysis and use self-awareness to narrow down choices to reasonable, manageable options.
4. Design and carry out a personal experiment or action plan that tests what works for you, balancing exploration with practical limits.

What Is It?

You've likely heard sayings like: "I've got to see it to believe it," "Let the buyer beware," "Trust, but verify," or "Open to learning, careful in believing."

This kind of advice reminds us that while we should stay open-minded, we also need to be cautious of overly persuasive sales pitches and scrutinize anything that seems unbelievable.

Improving our wellbeing often starts with curiosity. We want to try something new to change our diet, exercise routine, or sleep habits, or even reconsider our careers. While curiosity sparks our thinking, we can quickly get lost in a vast sea of useless, sometimes harmful self-help misinformation.

Poor, even risky, advice comes at us from all directions, often conflicting, exaggerated, or cleverly presented to sell us the next miracle fix.

We're not lacking information; we're overwhelmed by it. The real challenge is learning to tell what's true from what's just background noise, what's helpful from marketing hype, and what's effective from what's being sold as the latest fix for all our problems.

That's where *Prove It to Yourself* comes in.

It's about being informed and practicing self-mastery—trying out our own methods, paying close attention, and discovering what works for us. Not just in theory. Not based on someone else's story. In our bodies, minds, and lives.

Progress won't come from endlessly chasing trends, but from making safe, sensible, and sustainable choices—choices that suit our unique circumstances and pass real-life tests.

Why It Matters

We're bombarded daily by a relentless stream of marketing—through social media feeds, email blasts, commercials, and the endless scroll of must-try hacks.

This constant barrage does more than overwhelm us; it erodes our ability to tell practical solutions from hype. And here's a real danger: what has changed someone else's life might do nothing for us—or worse, it could set us back.

Our bodies, resources, and environments are not interchangeable. There is no one-size-fits-all solution.

"Proving it" separates being swept up by trendy fads from living with self-mastery. Instead of impulsively trying every new strategy, we slow down, ask tough questions, and test ideas against our real-life experiences.

By doing this, we safeguard our time, energy, money, and wellbeing from being squandered—and we focus our resources on what aligns with our path forward.

Growth isn't a byproduct of exposure. It's the result of deliberate choices. Anyone can absorb noise; guided by self-mastery, we sort it, interpret it, and act on it. That's how raw input becomes information, how information becomes knowledge, and how knowledge drives real growth.

Practical Application.

An idea alone cannot bring about change, but it may hold potential.

Until we test it in our daily lives, it stays just a theory. Proving it requires embracing change, taking action, and seeing if an idea produces results for us. Results that matter to us in our specific situation, regardless of what the thing did or supposedly does for anyone else.

That process is informed by self-awareness. Without judgment or harsh self-criticism, we assess who we are, where we stand, and what we need or want to change. We reflect on our strengths, weaknesses, and values so we can make adjustments that align with who we are rather than conflict with it.

But having an idea and awareness still aren't enough. Practical applications need proof of concept—showing it works for us in our specific situation. That involves running experiments in our own lives, observing the results, and making changes based on real experience rather than hope, hype, or wishful thinking.

Think of a simple example: imagine we want to lose a few pounds. We've heard about a new diet trend that's supposed to "melt fat fast." Instead of jumping in headfirst and adopting the entire plan, we research it and, if it seems practical, try small, safe, incremental changes. Maybe that means cutting out processed snacks or adding more whole foods to our diet. Over the next two weeks, we can observe: Did our energy improve? Do our clothes feel looser? Did our mood change? Does it make a meaningful, measurable difference? Can this be maintained?

We now have evidence from our personal experience. We can keep what works, discard what doesn't, and avoid wasting time, effort, and money chasing someone else's miracle fix.

That's self-mastery in action: we're no longer depending on promises, popularity, or what's being marketed to us in the sea of misinformation; we're trusting our own lived results.

A change must show its value. If it offers tangible benefits—like more energy, clearer thinking, or increased satisfaction—it deserves a spot in our lives. If it doesn't, we let it go. By treating growth as a series of intentional experiments, we design an efficient and effective personal transformation plan—one that is testable, reliable, and uniquely ours.

Challenges and Pitfalls

When striving for self-improvement, we face a flood of options, information, and opinions—many of which are amplified by social media and marketing aimed directly at us. While the desire to better ourselves is motivating and fuels our efforts, it's neither practical nor effective to try every available stress management technique, diet plan, workout routine, or self-improvement strategy.

We don't pursue every opportunity we come across; instead, we make informed, strategic decisions based on who we are, where we are, and what we can handle effectively.

How can we move forward in identifying what works for us? The process starts with self-awareness and is driven by self-mastery. Before making any changes, it is important to reflect on our past experiences. What strategies have we tried before, and what were their results?

Then, what are our strengths and weaknesses related to this particular change? Do we understand what challenges we'll face, and are we prepared to handle the uncertainties involved?

Next, we identify actionable steps that are reasonable and manageable, considering our current abilities and circumstances. Which habits and routines should we temporarily relinquish to make room for this change? Can we realistically dedicate the necessary time, effort, and resources to sustain it?

To provide insight as we start our change, we look to Warren Buffett, one of the world's most renowned investors. His investment philosophy is simple: focus on what we know and understand. Buffett describes this as our "circle of competence," stating:[63]

> Intelligent investing is not complex, though that is far from saying that it is easy. What an investor needs is the ability to correctly evaluate selected businesses. Note that word "selected": You don't have to be an expert on every company, or even many. You only have to be able to evaluate companies within your circle of competence. The size of that circle is not very important; knowing its boundaries, however, is vital.

Buffett's idea goes beyond financial investment—it also relates to our personal development.

When considering major life changes—like adopting a new diet, starting an exercise routine, or changing jobs—it's important to evaluate our circle of competence. This involves reflecting on our experiences and assessing our knowledge, skills, and habits related to the change. We also think about how much more we need to learn about it, all while being aware of our limitations.

By understanding what we know and what we don't, we build the foundation for meaningful and sustainable progress. While we don't need to be experts in every aspect of a change before starting, having enough understanding helps us make informed decisions and reduce unnecessary risks.

Well informed by self-awareness and guided by self-mastery, we start with what we know and understand, manage risk properly, and grow our knowledge and experience accordingly.

Timeless Wisdom

Like the other principles we've discussed, the idea of proving it to yourself has a written history that dates back thousands of years.

A well-known framework for seeking knowledge comes from the French philosopher René Descartes, who lived from 1596 to 1650, and famously said, "I think, therefore I am." In summary, his four rules for acquiring knowledge and pursuing truth are:[64]

1. Accept nothing as true until we clearly recognize it to be so.
2. Solve a problem systematically by breaking it up into smaller parts.
3. Proceed with understanding the parts from the simplest and gradually work towards the more complex ones.
4. Review everything thoroughly to ensure that nothing is left out.

The first rule when considering a self-help change emphasizes the importance of skepticism and critical thinking. We shouldn't immediately accept anything we're told or have read as true; instead, we should scrutinize and question it until we're confident it's valid for the specific change we're considering. It encourages us to approach problems with both an open mind and a readiness to question everything.

Together, these four rules act as a useful guide for navigating large amounts of information, helping us find what is meaningful related to the specific change we need or want.

For an earlier historical reference, we look back to Confucius, who emphasized thoroughly investigating and understanding a thing before forming beliefs about it. He taught:[65]

> Learning without thought is labor lost;
> thought without learning is perilous.

This passage emphasizes the importance of both learning and critical thinking. Confucius suggests that simply accepting information without reflection or comprehension is pointless, and that thinking deeply without a solid knowledge base can be dangerous.

We conclude with a profoundly meaningful, timeless reminder. Although the world has changed greatly over thousands of years, it remains remarkably the same in how we are continuously persuaded, influenced, badgered, tricked, or pressured to believe something despite contradictions.

Importantly, given the widespread disparities and resulting confusion about what will work for us in our pursuits, we need to discover it for ourselves. This sound advice comes from one of the wisest of all.

The Buddha's *Kalama Sutta* is a well-known speech he delivered to the Kalama people of Kesaputta. At that time, the Kalamas were confused by at least 62 philosophical systems and the contradictory spiritual teachings of various rival teachers.

Seeking guidance on what to believe amidst these philosophical and religious dilemmas, they turned to the Buddha for advice. In response, the Buddha didn't give them a ready-made answer. Instead, he encouraged them to question everything—even his own words.

Kalama Sutta (Kesamutta Sutta)[66]

> Do not believe in anything simply because you
> have heard it.
>
> Do not believe in traditions because they have
> been handed down for many generations.
>
> Do not believe in anything because it is spoken
> and rumored by many.
>
> Do not believe in anything simply because it is
> found written in your religious books.
>
> Do not believe in anything merely on the authority
> of your teachers and elders.
>
> But after observation and analysis, when you find
> that anything agrees with reason and is conducive
> to the good and benefit of one and all, then
> accept it and live up to it.

The Kalama Sutta reminds us that the real test of any self-improvement practice is not authority or tradition, but whether it proves beneficial in our own direct experience. Transformation must be lived, not merely believed.

This advice remains just as relevant today as it was 2,500 years ago. Just as the Kalamas faced a constant barrage of competing voices, we also live in a world overwhelmed by social media gurus, marketing-driven fads, and contradictory expert opinions.

What seems like a modern crisis of information overload is actually a long-standing human challenge. But the solution stays the same: practice discernment, trust our lived experience, and verify what works for us.

Getting caught up in the hype around the latest self-help breakthrough can be easy. Maybe it will work for us, maybe not. Before deciding to pursue something, we research and evaluate what it claims to do and see if it has potential benefits for us in our situation.

"Ehipassiko," the Buddha said, "Come and see."

That's the best advice for pursuing the change we need or want. As with any idea or suggestion, it all comes down to learning for ourselves. What sounds reasonable? What change might work? And what sounds far-fetched?

Gather the facts, evaluate our unique circumstances, trust our instincts, and then verify for ourselves.

Anecdote: Prove It

Self-improvement involves a deliberate, self-guided process that helps us move from our current position to our desired destination. To get there, we rely on our personal preferences, tendencies, abilities, and resources.

To illustrate, let's consider a daily commute to and from work. Because of our unique circumstances, this example shows how we choose what works best for us among the options, regardless of what might be effective for others.

Let's further imagine that we live and work in a large, crowded, busy, and costly metropolitan area with many commuting options— like Washington, D.C. Given our situation, we want to find out which commute option is best for us.

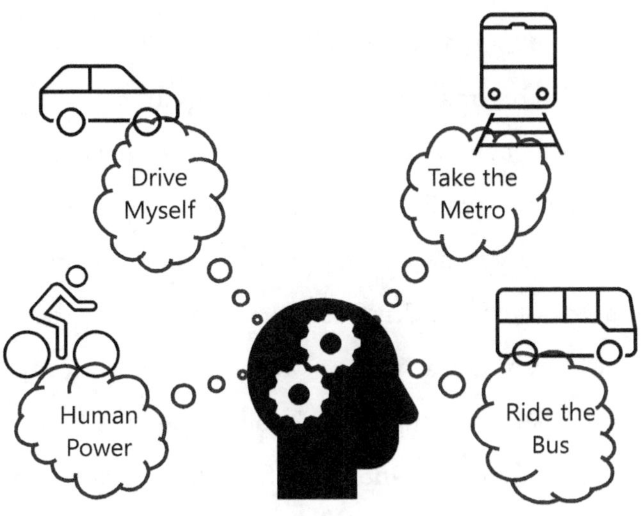

Figure 6.1 How am I going to commute?

The following is based on real-life experiences I witnessed daily—experiences that left lasting stress on the people I worked with, those who worked for me, and myself. For nearly twenty years as a frontline supervisor and manager in the Washington, D.C., metropolitan area, I observed the same pattern repeat across job titles, backgrounds, and departments. Before the workday even began, many of us were already exhausted from battling the same relentless, invisible enemy: the commute.

What seemed like a simple drive to the office could turn into an exhausting test of patience and endurance. Miles of brake lights illuminated the Beltway, I-95, I-66, and everywhere else, with cars crawling forward as if time had stopped. While listening to traffic updates on the radio, we hoped a major accident blocking all lanes of traffic was happening elsewhere, or at least in the lanes going in the opposite direction. Our hands cramped from gripping the wheel, our shoulders tensed, and our eyes darted between the clock and the unmoving line of traffic—with every minute lost, our anxiety about being late grew.

And that was just the drive to work. The same process was repeated on the way home, which was often even worse, especially on the last workday before a long federal holiday weekend.

Public transit didn't guarantee relief. It often meant rushing to the subway or bus stop, waiting a long time, and worrying whether the train or bus would arrive on time. Even when it did, it might be full, leaving only space to stand shoulder to shoulder and brace against every jolt. Or, making us wait for the next one.

By the time we got to the office, our patience was gone, and our energy was low. Snapping tempers, strained focus, and fatigue became the unspoken start of each day.

For many, the commute was never just a minor inconvenience. It stole our sleep, interrupted family dinners, and wore down our resilience. Over weeks, months, and years, this stress built up into chronic fatigue, affecting not only productivity and workplace culture but also our overall health and wellbeing.

The truth is clear: a tough commute doesn't just mark the start and end of the workday; it impacts every part of life. It affects how we act at work and when we get back home, making us wonder how much longer we can handle a difficult commute.

As we discussed in the introduction, it's important to recognize and tackle these stressors. In areas where traffic and transit problems are well-known, having a sustainable commute isn't a luxury; it's vital for maintaining balance, health, and the ability to thrive.

Clearly, for those of us who commute to work, we need to find an option that best fits our circumstances. Let's examine some of those options in the Washington, D.C., area.

Many commuters choose to drive themselves to and from work. This approach is convenient because it gives them greater flexibility in their schedule, allowing them to choose when to leave home, which route to take, where to park, and when to return.

Others prefer using the Metro whenever possible. This might include driving to the station and parking, or walking or biking there if convenient, then taking the subway to the stop closest to their workplace, and finally walking or taking a local bus from that stop to the office.

Some people choose a commuter rail system. This option is perfect for those whose starting point is far from a convenient Metro station but who still prefer using a rail line to get to work. Similar to the Metro, this involves traveling from home to the commuter rail parking lot, taking the train to the nearest stop to the workplace, and then, for the final part of the commute, walking, catching a bus, or riding the subway to the office.

Many people choose to vanpool to work if enough regular riders share the same destination—such as the Pentagon. This might involve driving to a designated parking lot and then boarding a van that picks up other passengers bound for the same workplace. One major benefit of vanpooling is that the driver can use high-occupancy vehicle (HOV) lanes, which are often less crowded than regular lanes. This reduced congestion can lead to significantly faster commutes compared to non-HOV lanes, making it a real time-saver.

One innovative way I learned to commute was by driving a car with a bicycle mounted on it. Commuters then park their vehicles near the office, where free on-street parking is still available. From there, they ride their bikes the rest of the way to work. This option, for example, avoids paying parking fees at the office lot, which can be expensive, and provides a great way to exercise at the start and end of their workday.

Another option unique to the Washington, D.C. commuting area is the "slug line." Commuters drive to and park in designated lots, then line up to wait for a ride with a driver they often do not know. With this "instant carpool" option, the driver picks up multiple passengers headed to the same destination, such as the Pentagon, allowing them to use HOV lanes. The return trip works similarly—stand in line, wait for a driver going to the central meeting point where you parked your car, and once enough passengers are on board, drive through the HOV lanes to the drop-off location.

It may seem odd at first to see strangers sharing a car just to use the HOV lanes, but it actually works. Plus, it's a free ride for the passengers. I've often heard that the success of this unusual commuter system is due to the government not regulating it. There might be some truth to that.

Of course, weather permitting, those who live close enough to the workplace can walk or bike to the office.

Given this sample of commuting options, which one would you choose?

- Driving yourself to and from the workplace.
- Using the subway system all the way or in part.
- Using a commuter rail all the way or in part.
- Using a vanpool.

- Driving a car most of the way and then riding your bike for the rest.
- Relying on the slug line.
- Walking or riding a bicycle.

My guess for your answer: ***It depends.***

Your choice depends on where you live and work, as well as other destinations you need to reach during your commute, such as dropping off and picking up children at school, your spouse's or partner's work or school schedule, how much time you have for it, what you can afford or are willing to spend, and what makes you feel safe and comfortable, among many other considerations.

In short, your personal work–life situation will ultimately determine which commute is best for you.

In this example, there is no one best solution for every commuter. Driving alone works for some, but not everyone; similarly, public transportation, vanpools, walking, or biking are options for certain people, but not all.

In summary: To each their own.

Self-improvement, like choosing a commute, isn't a one-size-fits-all approach. In a team of 25 people reporting to the same office, everyone tried to arrive on time, yet each selected an option based on their personal work-life circumstances. There were 25 different daily stories. Others' choices can offer insight, but they can't replace individual judgment. The responsibility—and the decision—rests with each of us, alone.

When we need or want to change, it's up to us to learn and decide what works best for us, based on who we are and where we are. For our personal growth, we explore, evaluate, safely experiment, and ultimately discover what "best" means, amid the endless and sometimes unrealistic self-help ideas available.

On a related note, during the years I worked in the same office complex in the Washington, D.C. area, I lived in four different, distant locations. From these four starting points, I tried many of the methods listed above. Eventually, I settled on another commuting option that worked best for me—but I don't recommend it to anyone.

In my experience, it greatly enhanced my work–life balance. I'll share more about my commuting journey and why I chose what I did in *Phase Three: Plan and Execute*.

Takeaways

- Ideas can be helpful and worth considering, but taking action gets results.
- To each their own: It's up to us to prove what works for us, given our unique situation.
- Nothing too much: We can become overwhelmed by sifting through endless options. Informed by self-awareness and guided by self-mastery, we narrow our possible choices to what's reasonable to explore, given who and where we are.

End of Module 6 – Explore Your Options

Your daily habits and routines impact your energy, focus, and overall wellbeing. Self-mastery involves noticing what can help you thrive, experimenting with change, and reflecting on what works best for you. When working toward self-improvement, treat changing habits and routines as personal experiments. Make one safe, informed adjustment at a time, observe how it affects you, and refine it based on your experience.

Given a specific goal you're working toward, what will you learn about, try, and decide if it works for you, considering your unique circumstances?

Crucially, knowing what doesn't work can be just as important as knowing what does.

Get informed and keep in mind that the only failure is the failure to try.

Exploring Self-Improvement Strategies

When looking for scientifically supported self-help wellness strategies to improve our diet, physical activity, or sleep habits, for example, it's best to start with the most reputable and comprehensive sources available. Published "consensus statements" and "position stands" offer expert-backed summaries that synthesize extensive research into clear, science-based advice.

These are reliable starting points that can help us make evidence-based decisions rather than relying on trends or life hacks. However, they don't cover every self-help topic we might look into, so think of them as a useful initial reference point on our path to self-improvement, not the final stop.

Once we understand what science generally supports through consensus statements and position stands, we can confidently explore more about what might work best for us in our unique situation. Subsequent sources for our personal research include government websites that offer practical, accessible guidance for daily use. Next, we have scientific literature, which provides deeper insights and emerging viewpoints, while reputable health systems and professional associations offer clinically grounded advice. Additional sources—such as books, podcasts, and blogs—can add personal flavor but should supplement, not replace, evidence-based information.

This layered approach ensures both reliability and relevance in our self-improvement journey.

Consensus Statements and Position Stands

These are reliable summaries of scientific evidence compiled by expert organizations after careful reviews of research on topics like nutrition, exercise, and sleep.

Consensus statements represent the collective interpretation of current evidence by a panel of experts, often following a structured review and discussion. Position stands go further by providing specific recommendations or guidelines for practice, policy, or public health based on that evidence. Both serve as reputable sources for understanding what the scientific community currently agrees on—and what actions are recommended in light of that consensus.

When exploring wellness topics to develop our self-improvement strategies, these sources are among the most reliable—they summarize studies into clear, unbiased advice that can guide personal decisions.

Of course, what matters is what works best for us, given our unique situation—and that's what we're exploring. If consensus statements and position stands on our self-help topic are available, we can start learning more through well-established, evidence-based guidance that ensures our testing or customization is grounded in the best current science.

For example, to better understand the importance of adequate sleep for our physical and mental health, here we have the first part of a joint consensus statement from the American Academy of Sleep Medicine (AASM) & Sleep Research Society (U.S.).[67]

> Adults should sleep <u>7 or more</u> hours per night on a regular basis to promote optimal health. Sleeping less than 7 hours per night on a regular basis is associated with adverse health outcomes, including weight gain and obesity, diabetes, hypertension, heart disease and stroke, depression, and increased risk of death. Sleeping less than 7 hours per night is also associated with impaired immune function, increased pain, impaired performance, increased errors, and greater risk of accidents.

As a reminder, consensus statements and position stands on narrow self-improvement topics involving diet, exercise, and sleep are relatively limited compared to the broader range of available information—but this is a great place to start our research.

Sources for Personal Research on a Specific Self-Improvement Topic

Beyond consensus statements and position stands, the available information is vast and seemingly endless, making it overwhelming and discouraging to navigate. As we develop self-mastery, we're reminded that impulsively following online clickbait or trends just because everyone else does it can be risky—and possibly dangerous.

But we don't have to try to sort through everything we will find—or even most of it. Or even much of it.

Following is a ranked list of sources for conducting personal research on wellness.

Conclusion

By now, you've explored the inner landscape of transformation—moving from awareness to action, from intention to integrity. You've learned that skillful change isn't about controlling everything; it's about focusing on what you can control: your thoughts, choices, mindset, actions, purpose, and health, and strategically influencing others and your environment.

Phase One: Let's Bring It All Together

Awareness opens the door. Humility keeps it open. And health sustains the journey. Self-mastery weaves these practices into wisdom—reminding us that wisdom is not a destination, but a way of life.

Introduction: Change is shaped by who we are and the circumstances around us, and lasting growth comes from choosing to work with both—not just wishing, but taking action. By understanding ourselves, adjusting to and influencing our environment, and pursuing balance through intentional effort, we move from needing or desiring change to sustaining it.

Module 1: Practice self-awareness. You can't change what you refuse to see. Awareness takes courage—the moment you choose clarity over comfort. Keep practicing reflection and honest feedback. Know your

Sources for Personal Research on Self-Help Wellness Topics

Rank	Source Type	Examples
1	Consensus Statements and Position Stands	American Academy of Sleep Medicine (AASM) & Sleep Research Society; American College of Sports Medicine
2	Government or Intergovernmental Health Agencies	World Health Organization (WHO), National Institutes of Health, including (1) MedLinePlus--for the general public, (2) NIH Health Information--for the public and patients, and (3) PubMed--for researchers, clinicians, and students
3	Professional & Scientific Organizations (may require membership)	APA PsycNet, American Academy of Sleep Medicine (AASM), American College of Sports Medicine (ACSM), Academy of Nutrition and Dietetics (AND)
4	Peer-Reviewed Journals & University Research Centers (may require membership)	JAMA, The Lancet, The New England Journal of Medicine
5	Reputable Health Systems & Academic Medical Centers (many with open, public access)	Mayo Clinic, Cleveland Clinic, Johns Hopkins Medicine, Harvard Health Publishing
6	Established News Outlets with Science Desks (may require membership)	Scientific American, BBC Science & Environment, New York Times Health
7	Books, Commercial Blogs, Influencers, or Testimonials	Use cautiously; verify claims using higher-ranked sources above.

Table 6.1 Sources for Personal Research

Understanding the Hierarchy of Research Evidence

As we do personal research to improve our health, performance, or emotional wellbeing, we'll likely come across published scientific studies. Understanding how different types of evidence are ranked helps us distinguish stronger from weaker claims. The hierarchy of evidence, shown in the following table, helps us evaluate the relevance, scope, and size of research, enabling more confident decision-making.

Hierarchy of Evidence - Rank Ordered

Rank	Type of Research	Summary
1	Meta-Analyses & Systematic Reviews	Combine data from multiple studies to identify consistent patterns and reduce bias.
2	Randomized Controlled Trials (RCTs)	Participants are randomly assigned to test or control groups; gold standard for testing cause and effect.
3	Cohort Studies	Follow large groups of people over time to track habits and outcomes.
4	Case-Control Studies	Compare individuals with and without a condition; useful for identifying risk factors.
5	Cross-Sectional Studies	Examine a population at one point in time; good for prevalence, not causality.
6	Case Reports / Case Studies	Describe individual or small group cases; informative but anecdotal.

Table 6.2 Hierarchy of Evidence

Finally, as subparts of government websites, two other reputable repositories maintained by the U.S. Department of Defense can be useful, especially for further research on many of the specific topics covered in this book.

The Defense Technical Information Center (DTIC)

DTIC serves as the DoD's central repository for scientific, technical, engineering, and research information. It offers access to a wide array of reports, studies, academic papers, and other publications from military, government, and educational researchers.[68]

For developing our self-help strategies, DTIC can be a valuable resource because it offers credible, research-based publications on topics such as self-improvement, stress management, self-awareness, resilience, human performance, values, cognitive biases, and leadership—some of the areas that military researchers examine to enhance planning, decision-making, and physical and mental readiness.

Alongside modern research, DTIC provides references to timeless wisdom from many of the great thinkers featured in this book. Here, you'll find discussions, analyses, and ideas from ancient Chinese philosophers like Lao Tzu and Sun Tzu—focusing, for example, on leadership and the power of *wu-wei*—as well as Confucian principles on ethics and harmony. The collection also includes commentary and insights on Western philosophers such as Aristotle, Socrates, and Plato, as well as on Stoic teachers such as Epictetus and Marcus Aurelius.

Beyond philosophy, you'll find references to psychologists whose work has influenced modern personal development—including Lewin on motivation, Maslow on self-actualization, Frankl on meaning, and Jung on the unconscious.

Exploring DTIC can deepen your understanding of how enduring ideas connect to contemporary science and self-improvement, showing that wisdom, from antiquity to the present, guides growth and resilience.

In summary, DTIC provides:

- Evidence-based insights rooted in psychological and behavioral research.
- Access to declassified and publicly available studies on human performance, resilience, and mental and physical fitness.
- Free, searchable content for anyone interested in understanding the science, personal experiences, and timeless wisdom behind practical decision-making, leadership, and personal growth, among other topics.

What makes DTIC unique is that much of its research is derived from active members of the U.S. military—such as senior-ranking students in capstone leadership and strategy programs—who have tested these principles, often under extraordinary pressure. Their work blends academic rigor with lessons learned in the most demanding real-world environments, from combat zones to crisis situations.

The result is a collection of insights on topics like focus, adaptability, leadership, resilience, and emotional control that extend far beyond the battlefield. It provides a rare perspective on human performance—one often rooted in frontline combat experience, discipline, and the desire for excellence. When we seek ways to become physically or mentally stronger, think more clearly, or lead more effectively, that view can be both humbling and deeply inspiring.

The Army Publishing Directorate (APD)

The APD provides a wide range of proven strategies to help you think, lead, and act more effectively. Army doctrine is organized into three levels: Army Doctrine Publications (ADPs), Field Manuals (FMs), and Army Techniques Publications (ATPs)—each offering a different perspective.[69]

ADPs outline the Army's core principles and leadership philosophy, making them ideal for exploring mindset, values, and strategic thinking. FMs convert those principles into structured methods for training, planning, and execution, while ATPs offer flexible, situation-specific techniques for accomplishing tasks under extreme pressure.

Army publications compile decades of leadership experience, research, and real-world practice into clear, actionable guidance for developing self-improvement strategies, including self-management, performing under pressure, building resilience, and leading others effectively. For example:[70]

- Leadership: Manuals like *Army Doctrine Publication (ADP) 6-22, Army Leadership and the Profession,* and *Field Manual (FM) 6-22, Developing Leaders,* discuss topics such as self-awareness, open-mindedness, personal biases, resilience, values, decision-making, intellect, and building trust—skills equally important in business, education, and everyday life.

- Fitness and Resilience: *FM 7-22, Holistic Health and Fitness,* offers an integrated framework for the Army's five domains of physical, nutritional, mental, spiritual, and sleep readiness—the foundation for all Soldier readiness initiatives—grounded in behavioral science and designed for sustainability.

- Professional Growth: Throughout Army doctrine, a consistent theme of adaptability, self-awareness, continuous improvement, and ethical leadership is emphasized—core habits of effective people in any field.

The Big Difference

What sets the Army Publishing Directorate apart from the other repositories previously listed is that its materials are not just theoretical ideas or optional reading—they are directive, authoritative, and crucial for executing military leadership.

These publications affect the daily decisions and actions of nearly one million active, Reserve, and National Guard Soldiers. They are designed to be referenced, followed, practiced, and incorporated into daily Army life.

Army doctrine condenses complex principles into clear, actionable guidance. It prepares leaders at all levels to make decisions that directly impact mission success and the wellbeing of their Soldiers. By following these directives, leaders foster discipline, consistency, and trust—key qualities of a force ready to operate under pressure.

While these publications are written for Soldiers—typically aged 17 to 55, physically and mentally fit, and trained for high-stakes environments—self-help readers will find a wealth of thoroughly tested frameworks for growth. These materials were developed under conditions where clarity, consistency, and performance are essential for operational success.

For those seeking disciplined, proven, and "in use today" methods of leadership, decision-making, and personal development, the APD provides a platform where theory and practice merge—and excellence is crucial.

As the Army saying goes: When in doubt, look it up. The Army Publishing Directorate is the primary source for that.

Final Tip: The Rule of 3 – A Simple Way to Stay Better Informed

The Rule of 3 is a straightforward, useful tool for slowing your decision-making process and thinking more clearly before taking action. When you're considering changes to your diet, exercise routine, sleep habits, or other self-improvement efforts, this rule helps you make confident, intentional choices—rather than jumping into the latest trend or a quick fix.

One: Explore at least three credible options. Avoid settling on the first promising idea. Instead, identify three realistic, evidence-based alternatives and compare them side by side. This encourages you to pause and evaluate, rather than just react. Ask yourself which options best align with your goals, preferences, health considerations, and lifestyle.

Two: Ask the same three key questions about each option. These questions base your decisions on facts and help you focus on long-term consistency rather than short-term motivational spikes. For each option you evaluate, pause and ask:

- What evidence supports the overall effectiveness of this option for the change I am pursuing?
- Is it safe, practical, and sustainable for me personally, considering my unique situation?
- How can I track if it's working?

Three: Verify the evidence for each option by cross-checking at least three separate, trustworthy, and knowledgeable sources. Confirm your findings by reviewing reliable information such as government websites, scientific summaries, professional guidelines, and expert commentary. When multiple credible sources agree, it shows that you are making a strong, well-supported choice.

Why the Rule of 3 Works

The structure of the Rule of 3 forces a brief, meaningful pause in your decision-making process. It gives you space to weigh alternatives, challenge assumptions, and make choices that feel both informed and aligned with your values. It also reduces second-guessing later, because you know you acted on research rather than impulse or marketing hype.

Example: Choosing a Diet Plan Using the Rule of 3

Imagine you're trying to adopt a healthier eating pattern. Instead of focusing on just one diet you've recently heard of, you narrow it down to three strong options to explore further, such as the:

- **DASH Diet:** One of the most clinically validated eating patterns for lowering blood pressure and improving heart health. It prioritizes fruits, vegetables, whole grains, and low-fat dairy—habits consistently linked to better long-term outcomes.

- **Mediterranean Diet:** Backed by decades of global research, this whole-food approach (olive oil, fish, legumes, vegetables) is associated with reduced cardiovascular risk and improved longevity.

- **Mayo Clinic Diet:** A research-driven, habit-based program designed to build sustainable weight-management behaviors. It focuses on long-term lifestyle change rather than short-term restriction.

Next, evaluate each option against the others by asking the same three essential questions:

- **What's the evidence?** All three eating patterns—the DASH Diet, the Mediterranean Diet, and the Mayo Clinic Diet—are supported by reputable research. DASH and the Mediterranean Diet have particularly strong clinical evidence for cardiovascular benefits, while the Mayo Clinic Diet is grounded in behavioral science and long-term weight-management research.

- **Is it safe, practical, and sustainable for me?** All three are considered safe for most people. The DASH and Mediterranean diets may require more food preparation and fresh ingredients, while the

Mayo Clinic Diet emphasizes habit formation, which some may find easier to integrate into daily life.

- **How can I track my progress?** Regardless of the plan you choose, you can monitor your progress by tracking energy levels, digestion, weight changes, blood pressure (if relevant), or how consistently you follow the plan each week.

Finally, verify your findings by cross-checking them against three trustworthy sources—such as government websites, peer-reviewed research, and reputable health systems guidelines—to ensure accuracy. If, for example, three different credible sources indicate that a specific diet plan best fits your preferences and health goals, you can proceed with more confidence.

Applying the Rule of 3 consistently helps you become a better-informed decision-maker. With targeted research from reputable sources, you can often find as much—or more—useful information than what someone is trying to sell you.

Putting It All Together

To make informed, safe, and effective decisions about improving your wellbeing:

- Evaluate the source. Trust government or professional organizations over commercial websites.
- Assess the level of evidence. When reviewing research, examine consensus statements and position stands, consult government publications, and seek out systematic reviews and randomized controlled trials (RCTs).

- Seek consensus. Apply the Rule of 3. When multiple expert groups agree, their conclusions are more likely to be reliable.
- Stay curious but skeptical. Science evolves; remain open to learning while demanding credible evidence to support your specific self-improvement goals.
- Nothing too much. As we've seen throughout this book, a common pitfall is overthinking a topic and then getting stuck in analysis paralysis, making little to no meaningful progress. To achieve a change you need or want, you have to do more than think about it.

By following this process, you can distinguish science-backed strategies from temporary fads—and make safe, effective decisions that support your goals and wellbeing.

Next Up

As we finish this first book on developing self-mastery—the "P" in the behavioral formula—let's take a moment to highlight an important reminder about our overall wellbeing.

Wherever you are in your change journey, please do this for yourself.

Module 7: Schedule Health Checkups

If I am not for myself, who is for me? But if I am for my own self only, what am I? And if not now, when?—Hillel the Elder[71]

Learning Objectives: By the end of this module, you will be able to:

1. Monitor and record your baseline health metrics to assess your wellbeing and identify needed changes early.
2. Identify and access free or affordable healthcare resources when needed, demonstrating how to seek support beyond self-care to maintain your health.
3. Design and implement a personal health routine that includes regular checkups and ongoing monitoring, aligning daily actions with long-term wellness goals.

Disclaimer: The information provided below is for informational purposes only and should not be considered medical advice. It does not diagnose or treat illnesses or diseases, nor does it recommend specific treatment plans or exam schedules.

Please consult a licensed professional for personalized medical, mental health, vision, or dental advice and necessary treatment.

Why It Matters

Two thousand years ago, Hillel the Elder shared a universal truth: caring for others begins with caring for ourselves. Self-preservation isn't selfish—it's the foundation for giving back.

Before we can help others, we need to be strong enough to do so. Using a common self-help analogy, during the pre-flight safety briefing on an airplane, we're told that if the pilot deploys oxygen masks in an emergency, we should put ours on first before helping others. The reason is simple: if we lose consciousness, we can't assist anyone else.

The same idea applies in daily life—neglecting our health, skipping checkups, or ignoring stress can quietly take us out of action.

Hillel's wisdom and the airline metaphor share a single message: self-care isn't about isolation but about being ready. To fulfill your higher purpose, you must protect the vessel that carries it—yourself.

Understanding and regularly checking your baselines is like knowing your car's dashboard readings. You can tell when everything is running smoothly and when something might need attention. Without that knowledge, small issues can go unnoticed until they turn into major problems.

A single checkup can be the first step toward preventing health issues and building long-term wellness.

If you've served in the military, for example, you understand the importance of routine physicals, vision tests, and dental checkups. These aren't optional—they are mandatory. They are a vital part of staying prepared. And the checkups are strictly enforced.

Yes, scheduling and attending appointments require time, effort, and sometimes money. Still, it's one of the best investments we can make in ourselves.

The bottom line: you don't need to wait until something feels wrong.

By committing to regular checkups—whatever regular means for your circumstances—you demonstrate to yourself that your long-term wellbeing is worth the effort today.

Although not everyone has easy access to routine checkups covered by health insurance, in the United States, for example, many free or low-cost options are available for those who want to monitor their health without significant expense.

Practical Application

Accessible healthcare resources can include:

- Community Health Clinics: Many local clinics provide free or low-cost health screenings, including essential services like blood pressure checks, cholesterol tests, and immunizations.
- Local Health Departments often offer screenings, immunizations, and wellness programs at lower costs.
- Federally Qualified Health Centers (FQHCs) provide primary care services, including preventive screenings, regardless of a person's insurance status or ability to pay.
- Retail pharmacies and health fairs: Some pharmacies offer walk-in health screenings, and community health fairs often provide free checkups.

A Sample of Key Health Checkups and Screenings

Physical Exam: Regular visits to a primary care provider (PCP) help monitor overall health, update vaccinations, and address medical concerns. Depending on gender, age, medical history, and other factors, components might include:

- Blood Pressure Check – Crucial for identifying hypertension, which can cause heart disease or stroke.
- Cholesterol Screening – A lipid panel helps evaluate the risk of heart disease.
- Blood Glucose Test – This is essential for detecting early signs of diabetes, especially for individuals at higher risk.
- Skin Cancer Screening – Regular dermatology exams help catch issues early, leading to better treatment results.
- Colorectal Cancer Screening – Recommended based on age and personal risk factors to identify problems early.

Vision Exam: Essential for detecting conditions like glaucoma, macular degeneration, and other age-related vision issues.

Dental Checkup: Regular cleanings and exams prevent gum disease and help detect dental problems early.

As we've learned throughout this book, even though there is a vast amount of information available about our wellbeing—and we can't and wouldn't want to sift through all of it—we have to start somewhere to find what's relevant to us in our unique situation.

A good place to visit is MedlinePlus, an advertisement-free and subscription-free service provided by the U.S. National Library of Medicine (NLM), which is the world's largest medical library and part of the National Institutes of Health (NIH).[72]

For example, when it comes to recommended adult checkups, search results provide specific information for the following age groups: 18–39, 40–64, and 65+. This includes particular health screenings for both women and men. The links to these recommendations also offer more detailed references for further research on topics of interest.

Challenges and Pitfalls

Phase One of this program builds self-mastery by developing awareness, habits, and routines that support personal growth. Mental health remains a crucial part of this journey.

But it's important to realize that while self-help can get us far, it cannot—and should not—handle everything.

Self-mastery practices can help alter habits and establish healthier routines. However, concerns about addiction or substance use are best handled by a licensed behavioral health professional.

Knowing when to seek help is a form of wisdom and strength. The path to growth includes learning to discern when we can move forward on our own—and when we need others' support. The following two tables list some of the professionals who can help.

Module 7: Schedule Health Checkups

Profession	Summary	Licensure / Certification
Psychiatrist	A medical doctor who completes medical school or osteopathic school and psychiatric residency to diagnose and treat mental illnesses, prescribe medication, and provide psychotherapy.	State medical license; board certification (an additional voluntary credential) is via the American Board of Psychiatry and Neurology (ABPN).
Psychologist	A clinical or counseling professional with a Ph.D. or Psy.D. who performs psychological testing, diagnosis, and psychotherapy.	State psychology license; Examination for Professional Practice in Psychology (EPPP); board certification (a voluntary credential) is via the American Board of Professional Psychology (ABPP).
Psychiatric-Mental Health Nurse Practitioner (PMHNP)	An advanced practice registered nurse (APRN), with additional training in mental health, who diagnoses and treats psychiatric conditions.	Registered Nurse (RN) + Nurse Practitioner (NP) license; national certification via American Nurses Credentialing Center (ANCC).
Licensed Clinical Social Worker (LCSW)	A master's-level clinician providing therapy, case management, and social systems support.	State LCSW license; supervised clinical hours; Association of Social Work Boards (ASWB) Clinical Exam.
Mental Health Nurse Case Manager	A registered nurse (RN) who provides clinical case management for individuals with mental health or psychiatric conditions.	Active RN license (state-specific requirements apply). Employer-defined experience in psychiatric or behavioral-health nursing.
Floor Nursing Staff (RN or Licensed Practical Nurse (LPN))	Nurses who provide daily care, medication administration, and safety monitoring in psychiatric settings	Registered Nurse (RN): Requires NCLEX-RN; Licensed Practical Nurse (LPN): Requires NCLEX-PN
Peer Support Specialist	An individual with lived experience of mental health recovery who provides mentorship and support.	Varies by state; typically credentialed through peer support training; licensure not required.

Table 7.1 Behavioral Health Professionals - Hospital / Clinical Setting

Profession	Summary	Licensure / Certification
Licensed Professional Counselor (LPC)	A master's-trained therapist offering talk therapy, emotional support, and coping skills training.	Licensure: State LPC license; supervised hours; National Counselor Examination (NCE) or National Clinical Mental Health Counseling Examination (NCMHCE).
Licensed Marriage and Family Therapist (LMFT)	A master's-level clinician specializing in relational therapy for couples, families, and individuals.	State LMFT license; supervised hours; Marriage and Family Therapy National Examination.
Certified Alcohol and Drug Counselor (CADC)	A specialist in substance use treatment, relapse prevention, and recovery support.	Certification: International Certification & Reciprocity Consortium (IC&RC) or National Association for Alcoholism and Drug Abuse Counselors (NAADAC); licensure varies by state.
Board Certified Behavior Analyst (BCBA)	A master's-level clinician applying Applied Behavior Analysis (ABA) to support individuals with developmental or behavioral challenges.	Certification: Board Certified Behavior Analyst (BCBA) via Behavior Analyst Certification Board (BACB); many states require additional licensure.
Faith-Based and Spiritual Care Providers	Professionals such as chaplains, theologians, and community spiritual leaders who offer emotional, ethical, and existential support grounded in religious or philosophical traditions.	While they are not typically licensed mental health clinicians, they play a vital role in helping individuals explore meaning, grief, identity, and hope, often complementing clinical care. Their training varies by role and tradition.

Table 7.2 Behavioral Health and Spiritual Care Professionals - Outside Hospital / Clinical Setting

Takeaways

- Prioritize your health by understanding and monitoring your baseline metrics.

- If needed, find free or low-cost healthcare resources nearby.

- Regular checkups empower you to manage your health and detect potential issues early.

- It's an investment in yourself that also benefits others who rely on you.
- Nothing too much: Informed by self-awareness and guided by self-mastery, we can accomplish a lot in life on our own. But there will be times when we need help. When that time comes, seek it.

strengths and weaknesses, and adjust accordingly. Awareness starts where denial ends.

Module 2: Suspend preconceptions. Growth requires humility. Every assumption you make can be a potential blind spot. Learn to pause before drawing conclusions. Ask: What if I don't know? What could I learn here? Openness encourages practical knowledge; humility transforms it into understanding.

Module 3: Focus on control. You can't control external circumstances, but you can control how you respond. Direct your energy inward—toward effort, learning, and persistence. The sphere of control is where confidence and peace reside. Strategically engage in your sphere of influence.

Module 4: Cultivate a change mindset. Change is not your enemy; stagnation is. Let go of the past, embrace the present, and shape the future with curiosity and intention. Flexibility is strength in motion.

Module 5: Find your purpose. Purpose gives meaning to struggle and direction to action. Keep refining it as you grow—it's a living thing, not a final answer. Your "why" keeps you grounded when life tests your resolve.

Module 6: Prove it to yourself. Don't accept self-help advice uncritically from any source. Gather information, test it, evaluate the results, and make adjustments. The best teacher you'll ever have is your own experience combined with reflection.

Module 7: Schedule health checkups. Even the strongest mindset weakens without physical fitness. Schedule regular checkups. Keep an eye on your baselines. Treat your body as your most critical system—because it is. As Hillel asks, consider: "If I am not for myself, who is for me?" You can't support others if your tank is empty.

Call to Action

Self-mastery isn't a one-time achievement—it's a daily practice. Every day, you face choices: drift or steer. React or respond. You can try to repeat yesterday or redesign today.

- Choose to lead yourself informed by awareness, openness, and care.
- Choose to make change your ally, rather than your adversary.
- Choose to demonstrate your potential—not to the world, but to yourself.
- The journey to mastery doesn't end here; it starts fresh every day you walk it.
- Starting today, work on developing the skill. Practice applying self-mastery to a personal change that is important to you.

Because if not you—who? And if not now—when?

Looking Ahead

Phase One focused on understanding and strengthening the *person*—your patterns of thought, emotion, habit, and self-regulation. That work matters. But it is incomplete on its own. No amount of insight or discipline can reliably overcome an environment that works against you.

Human behavior doesn't happen in a vacuum; it is shaped, limited, and reinforced by the systems, spaces, and social worlds we navigate every day. When progress stalls, the issue is often not a lack of motivation but a mismatch between who you are and the conditions around you.

Phase Two shifts our focus outward—to the environments that influence choice, effort, and opportunity. Here, change relies more on careful planning than on depending solely on internal willpower. By analyzing macro forces, daily micro-environments, and understanding psychological needs and desires, this phase turns challenges into strategic opportunities. With an emphasis on intentionally engaging with our environment, we harness the self-mastery developed in Phase One to navigate these dynamics effectively.

The goal is not to control the world, but to position yourself wisely within it—so growth becomes sustainable, self-efficacy strengthens, and progress no longer depends on constant self-correction. We'll explore:

- How context, culture, and systems influence behavior, opportunities, and perceived choices.
- Why some environments promote growth while others consistently hinder it, regardless of effort or motivation.
- How to evaluate fit—among yourself, your roles, and your environment—so that difficulty is understood properly instead of taken personally.
- How to select change strategies that are realistic, sustainable, and suited to your current situation.

By examining structural influences such as access, expectations, social norms, and daily contexts—without blame or judgment—you're encouraged to apply the self-mastery you gained in Phase One to problem-solving focused on the environment.

This shift redefines personal change as a design challenge instead of a moral one. Where Phase One asked, Who am I? and How do I change internally? Phase Two asks a different, equally important question: What needs to change around me for growth to happen naturally?

When you learn to strengthen P and strategically influence E, change no longer depends only on constant effort. Together, they establish a two-part model for transformation—from within and from without.

Your journey continues.

Let's Go!

The Story Behind the Lessons in Change

Before we can discuss readiness, discipline, or transformation, it is helpful to understand where those lessons were forged. The insights in this book series didn't come just from theory; they came from learning, application, experience, mistakes, hard-earned clarity, and the moments that forced a different way forward.

This is the story behind those lessons—the lived experience that shaped the principles you're exploring.

Forged by Four Decades of Continuous Change

Change was the only constant throughout both my careers. I didn't just face it—I was shaped by it. I survived change, adapted to it, learned from it, practiced it, and led it. And now, I teach it.

That journey didn't begin with confidence or foresight; it started out of necessity. The Army changed—often faster than I expected—and if I wanted to stay relevant, I had to adapt. There was no waiting for stability. Resisting change was pointless if I wanted to stay in the game.

1980s: When Adaptability Meant Survival

My active-duty career began in the late 1970s, initially driven more by realism than optimism about change. Essentially, I wanted a stable job, perhaps even a career, and was willing to work toward it.

The Army trained me to operate and maintain Vietnam-era tactical communications equipment—technology that defined operational readiness at the time. But within four years, just as I became highly skilled, the equipment became obsolete. I had to let go of everything I had learned, was good at, and enjoyed doing.

I was then retrained in a second specialty, working with decentralized "minicomputer" systems that automated logistics, personnel, and ammunition management. At that time, those systems were state-of-the-art. The training was extensive and thorough, and working with advanced computer technology was thrilling. I was part of fielding teams that installed, tested, "burned in," and serviced new capabilities at three sites in Korea and at Fort Bragg, North Carolina. I became skilled in all aspects of hardware, software, operations, troubleshooting, and maintenance, and was promoted to senior technician.

But it didn't last.

As with my first specialty, the equipment became obsolete after only a few years with the advent of the "microcomputer," now commonly known as the personal computer (PC). So, I had to pivot again.

Watching my hard-earned training, skills, and expertise fade into history twice in less than a decade taught me an important lesson:

competence alone isn't enough. No matter how technically skilled I became, staying relevant required continuous learning. Adaptability is what keeps you employable.

During that first decade, I was reacting to change. I was also learning to let go of skills I had just acquired, replace them with new ones, and adapt before the Army moved on without me. The Army didn't reward loyalty to tools or technologies. It rewarded adaptability, humility, and the willingness to evolve and lead. This reinforced the often-heard saying, "The Army didn't join you, you joined the Army, so get with the program."

I hadn't seen myself as a leader of change yet; I was just trying to survive it. But those early years shaped the mindset that would influence both careers: change is a force you need to learn to grow with. I was becoming skilled at understanding and managing continuous change.

1990s: Finding My Fit and Beginning to Lead Continuous Change

In the 1990s, adaptation shifted from mere survival to leading and driving organizational change. As desktop systems replaced the minicomputers I was just trained on, I moved into my third specialty: computer programming. As it turned out, this was my best fit.

Initially, I installed, enhanced, and maintained software systems for Army logistics, personnel, and ammunition management. Later, in Germany, I served as a senior systems administrator, managing local area networks on the Defense Data Network. I also helped establish and rapidly expand one of the Army's earliest email systems for the Hanau Military Community, which was then one of the largest area support groups in U.S. Army Europe (USAREUR). The new email capabilities greatly transformed our communications—locally, in-country, and worldwide. I adapted well to the role and found it an exciting and rewarding experience to introduce these new tools to the Army workforce.

Then everything changed dramatically, again.

The "Fall of the Berlin Wall" in November 1989 and the ceasefire in Desert Shield/Desert Storm operations in February 1991 led to significant geopolitical and DoD organizational changes. In the early 1990s, our local mission shifted from growth to supporting a rapid, large-scale reduction of Army forces in Europe, especially in Germany.

I transitioned from expanding networks and local email capabilities to dismantling them, while also developing and deploying innovative, locally unique software to help Soldiers transition out of Germany more quickly. Being part of that rapid, large-scale drawdown and witnessing the scope of military movement taught me something deeper: change like this doesn't just alter organizations, functions, and systems; it reshapes lives.

For example, in 1992 alone, over 70,000 Soldiers and 90,000 family members were redeployed to the U.S., as the Army nearly halved its infrastructure.[73] Facilitating that drawdown exposed me to the profound human toll and complexity behind large-scale organizational change.

Caught up in it, I was reassigned to a position in Alexandria, Virginia, where I was responsible for improving and maintaining the Army's noncommissioned officer (NCO) promotion model, which still operated on a legacy mainframe platform.

In this role, I was also trained in and led my first formal process improvement project, markedly increasing the accuracy of promotion forecasting and by-name promotion selection, thereby directly enhancing Army readiness. Playing a key role in efficiently managing the Army's enlisted end strength was exhilarating.

It was the best job I ever had on active duty, and Army enterprise-level software development was where I was making my greatest impact.

But it didn't last long.

Near the end of the decade, my career came to an abrupt halt when I was declared medically unfit for duty. After nearly twenty years of service, I had to let go of the identity I had built. The uniform was removed. My future remained as uncertain as ever.

Which meant I had to pivot again. And this was the biggest pivot of all—out of the Army, which had defined my entire adult life up to that point. What saved me wasn't luck; it was the mindset change I had been developing all along. I transitioned quickly into the private sector, then as an Army contractor hired for Year 2000 (Y2K) remediation of critical mainframe software, and eventually into a second civil-service career.

2000s: Learning to Lead Change at Scale

The 2000s signaled my transition from a technical expert to a burgeoning change practitioner.

After the successful Y2K remediation, I was promoted and given the responsibility to lead projects that upgraded the Army's enlisted and officer personnel management information systems—platforms used to distribute and assign hundreds of thousands of enlisted personnel, select thousands of NCO promotions each month, and support the career development of 80,000 active-duty officers.

In a short period, we reengineered and migrated legacy mainframe COBOL systems to a client-server architecture, then expanded functionality to a web-based environment, and then prepared for the move to an enterprise resource planning (ERP) platform. The pace was relentless. The overlaps were intentional. My teams and responsibilities kept growing. The complexities increased. And the stakes increasingly rose higher.

Leading these efforts taught me that change doesn't come from pressure—it comes from trust. I learned that pushing harder might move a project forward, but it often leaves people disillusioned and confused. Progress became more consistent when I shifted from managing tasks to leading people: understanding what motivates them, how organizations behave, and how to align energy and resources around a shared purpose.

That shift—from pushing through change to leading it—became the key difference between short-term wins and sustainable team performance, morale, and growth. It's the moment I realized that leadership isn't about forcing change harder; it's about becoming the kind of person others trust to navigate uncertainty.

But not everything was successful.

Over many years in three consecutive roles, I spent thousands of hours working on what was initially billed as the largest integrated human resources system in DoD history. After years of planning, coordination, design, development, and review of thousands of pages of documentation, and with a billion dollars invested, it became one of the biggest software failures ever. The department eventually canceled the program, mainly due to Army concerns.[74]

The failure was both devastating and formative. It taught me more about accountability and leadership than success ever did.

The takeaway lesson: Sometimes, adding more resources—regardless of how much—doesn't guarantee success.

Around the same time, another massive organizational transformation was underway. The 2005 Base Realignment and Closure (BRAC) Act mandated, among other measures, the relocation and consolidation of the Army Human Resources Command headquarters from Alexandria, Virginia, to Fort Knox, Kentucky.[75]

Similar to the Army drawdown in Europe a decade earlier, this was another large-scale relocation of people, processes, technology, and entire organizations.

On paper, the BRAC headline focused on facilities and realigning organizational charts. On the frontlines, however, it was about people. For the civilian employees in the command, we faced life-changing choices: move with the command to Kentucky and keep your job, or not. If not, then what? Find another local job, if any were available? Retire if you could? In this single example, thousands of careers, families, personal finances, and identities were suddenly in flux. Moving from Alexandria, Virginia, to Fort Knox, Kentucky, was a major upheaval, but so was losing your job. Whatever the case, a decision had to be made quickly.

As the Chief of Information Management for officer personnel, I served as a senior leader on the command's BRAC transition team. In this role, I helped plan the move while ensuring our worldwide mission continued without interruption. Equally important, we supported employees as they navigated uncertainty when no perfect options were available. BRAC taught me that leading through organizational change requires more listening than telling, more empathy than authority, all while maintaining a clear focus on the mission—especially when emotions run high and outcomes can't be softened.

And it reinforced the idea that when facing such a disruption, each person must decide what works best for them in their specific situation. Here was another example that there is no one-size-fits-all solution. We must each make our own informed choices based on who we are and where we are.

To each their own.

We'll revisit the lessons of BRAC in Phase Two because, like the drawdown of Army forces in Germany in the 1990s, BRAC 2005 showed the lasting and irreversible effects of major organizational change—and how we can apply those lessons as we plan our own personal change.

2010s: Treating Change as a Daily Discipline

Initially, I planned to keep my job and transfer with the command to Fort Knox rather than stay in Alexandria and risk being forced into an undesirable role—or, worse, failing to find another job at all. And with the sudden end of my active-duty career still fresh in my mind, I was once again facing personal, career, and financial uncertainty.

What this experience reinforced was that while we can't control the randomness of change, we can control our readiness for it. Opportunities don't come out of nowhere—they reveal themselves to those who have done the inner and outer work to be ready when the moment arrives.

As they say, luck favors those who are prepared.

During the hectic transitions of people, processes, and technology caused by BRAC, I was promoted to a senior leadership role at an Army agency unaffected by it. In my final two civil service positions, I was responsible for IT service and support for 35 geographically dispersed field offices nationwide and led improvements, maintenance, and daily global support for the Army's civilian personnel data system. In these roles, my focus shifted from managing change through individual projects to integrating change as a core operational practice.

The work was extensive: ongoing software delivery and maintenance, IT asset lifecycle management, software and hardware configuration management, development of command and agency policies and procedures extending nationally and globally, worldwide helpdesk operations, continuity of operations (COOP), and planning, organizing, and leading organizational change at the highest levels of the Army.

Every decision—software change packages, equipment lifecycle replacements, policies, and procedures—caused ripple effects across commands, installations, and the entire workforce.

Change had become a routine that required daily management. Leading at this scale demands patience, clarity, and a deep understanding and appreciation of organizational behavior and employee motivation. It involves treating change not as a one-time event to survive but as a daily discipline to practice. This is another effective change management strategy we'll examine in Phase Two, applying lessons from the operational and strategic levels to our planned personal change.

Over four decades, I transitioned from reacting to change out of necessity to intentionally leading it. I learned—sometimes the hard way—that relevance isn't something you achieve once. It's something you must continually earn.

In a Nutshell

Over the years, I've learned what works, what doesn't, and how to distinguish between the two.

What I share with you here isn't just theory. These are the same concepts, tools, and techniques I've tested and proven in real-world, high-stakes situations, refined through decades of personal reinvention and leading change at the highest organizational levels.

And I still use and teach them today.

The single most important lesson I've learned is this:

Don't get too comfortable.

Change is inevitable, but through self-mastery, you can become skilled at managing it. Good things happen more often to people who are prepared for them. Preparation opens opportunities that appear like luck from the outside.

Change Practitioner Summary

- 40 years of holding increasingly higher technical and leadership positions in information technology throughout two careers
- 3 military occupational specialties (MOS) on active duty; 9 different civilian job titles/occupational series after active duty
- 9 promotions, from the lowest Army enlisted rank to the highest grade in the federal civilian General Schedule (GS) pay system
- 25 assignments across 13 distinct duty locations, spanning three continents and eight U.S. states
- 24 moves / permanent changes of address

Education

- Master of Strategic Studies, U.S. Army War College, Carlisle Barracks, PA.

- Master of Public Administration, Troy University, Troy, Alabama.

- Graduate-level, practicum-based Certificate in Organizational Transformation, National Defense University, Fort McNair, Washington, D.C.

- Bachelor of Science in Computer Information Systems, Strayer University, Washington, D.C.

Resident Army Leadership Training

- U.S. Army War College

- Army Management Staff College: Sustaining Base Leadership and Management Program, Fort Belvoir, VA.

- Advanced Noncommissioned Officer (NCO) Course (ANCOC). Fort Gordon, GA.

- Basic NCO Course (BNCOC), Fort Gordon, GA.

- Primary Leadership Course (PLC), Fort Bragg, N.C.

Change Management Related Courses and Certifications

- Lean Six Sigma

- Total Quality Management (TQM)

- Project Management

- Knowledge Management

- Change Psychology

- Stress Management and Recovery

A Practice of Change Informed by Change Management Processes and Methodologies

Throughout my various roles, I've learned, applied, and succeeded with different formal approaches to planning, implementing, and sustaining change, depending on the mission. Some of these include:

- **SDLC** (Software Development Lifecycle): A systematic process for planning, designing, building, testing, deploying, and maintaining high-quality software, breaking complex projects into manageable phases.

- **Process Improvement** (Namely, TQM and Lean Six Sigma): Reduce variation, eliminate waste, and enhance reliability through data-driven analysis and ongoing feedback.

- **Project Management:** A disciplined framework for defining scope, managing resources, mitigating risk, and delivering outcomes within constraints.

- **IT Governance:** Frameworks for decision-making, accountability, and strategic alignment to ensure that technology investments, risks, and operations align with organizational objectives.

- **MDMP (Military Decision-Making Process):** A structured, analytical approach for making decisions and executing tasks amid uncertainty, risk, and constraints.

Military Occupational Specialty (MOS) Training

- 74F, Programmer/Analyst
- 34C, Decentralized Automated Service Support System (DAS3) Computer Repairer
- 31V, Tactical Communications Systems Operator/Mechanic

Appendix: DoD's Abundance

This discussion highlights two extremes in leveraging the department's abundant resources. On one end are large research and development projects—costly, high-profile, and risky—started with proof-of-concept funding to ensure the U.S. military remains the most capable in the world. At the other end are small local projects and programs that expand rapidly as resources become available, gradually increasing budgets and becoming permanent parts of daily operations.

On One End: DoD in Pursuit of What Will Be – Three DoD-funded Technologies That Changed the World

Three of the most influential technologies in global society today—electronic computers, GPS, and the Internet—were initially funded, developed, and expanded through DoD programs. Each now supports trillion-dollar industries and billions of users every day. And it all began with the military's pursuit of What Will Be.

The First Electronic General-Purpose Computer – ENIAC (U.S. Army Ordnance Department)[76]

In 1946, the U.S. introduced the Electronic Numerical Integrator and Computer (ENIAC), the first electronic general-purpose computer. Funded by the Army Ordnance Department during World War II to compute artillery tables, ENIAC, which was co-invented by John Mauchly and J. Presper Eckert at the University of Pennsylvania, proved that large-scale electronic computing was possible. However, the influence of ENIAC extended far beyond the Army.

In 1951, Mauchly and Eckert delivered their Universal Automatic Computer I (UNIVAC I), the first commercially available computer, to the U.S. Census Bureau. The development of UNIVAC I was based on their earlier research funded by the Army. The ENIAC project enabled important technical breakthroughs, such as high-speed electronic digital computing, vacuum-tube logic, and, later, stored-program design.

The debut of UNIVAC I demonstrated that the electronic computer could serve as a business tool, not only for military or scientific uses. This discovery accelerated IBM's entry into electronic computing and fueled the growth of the commercial computer industry.

By turning electronic computing from an Army research prototype into a commercial product, UNIVAC I helped boost productivity growth over decades and laid the foundation for the digital economy that fuels global innovation today.

Global Positioning System – GPS (U.S. Navy, DoD)[77]

The Soviet Union's launch of Sputnik, the world's first artificial satellite, in 1957 inspired scientists at Johns Hopkins University's Applied Physics Laboratory (APL) to use the Doppler Effect to track satellites, demonstrating that ground locations could be identified from satellite signals.

In 1958, the DoD's Advanced Research Projects Agency (ARPA, later DARPA) was established by President Eisenhower in response to Sputnik. They began developing Transit, the first global satellite navigation system. The first satellite for the Transit program was launched in 1960. The concept developed by Johns Hopkins University's APL proved capable of providing navigation to both military and commercial users, including the Navy's missile submarines. In the mid-1960s, the program was transferred to the Navy. By 1968, a constellation of 36 satellites was fully operational. Transit operated until 1996, when the Global Positioning System (GPS) replaced it.

GPS became accessible to civilians in 1983 when President Reagan authorized free public access to the satellite constellation after the tragic shootdown of Korean Airlines Flight 007 (KAL 007) as it strayed into Soviet airspace. The first commercial handheld GPS device appeared in 1989, followed by cellphone integration in 1999. In 2000, the U.S. eliminated "selective availability" and introduced three new civilian signals, dramatically improving accuracy overnight.

What began as a Cold War navigation system is now deeply embedded in transportation, logistics, emergency response, and everyday life everywhere.

The Birth of the Internet – ARPANET (ARPA / DARPA / Academia)[78,79]

The modern Internet began to develop in 1958, driven by psychologist and ARPA Program Manager Joseph Carl Robnett (J.C.R.) Licklider, alongside academic collaboration. Licklider envisioned the potential of interactive computing, or what he called "man-computer symbiosis."

With steady DoD funding, ARPA developed ARPANET, which sent its first host-to-host message on October 29, 1969, using "packet switching" between UCLA and the Stanford Research Institute. Throughout the 1970s, ARPANET served as a testing ground for email, the File Transfer Protocol (FTP), Telnet, mailing lists, and early online communities.

ARPANET's original goals included reliable communication and information sharing among geographically separated research facilities. A greater challenge soon arose: linking ARPANET to other network types beyond dedicated, hard-wired phone lines.

The department aimed to develop a mobile, durable, globally connected system to link planes, ships, and other assets. DoD experiments included SATNET (a U.S.–Europe satellite packet network) and packet radio networks based on ALOHANET principles (ALOHANET was a wireless system developed at the University of Hawai'i in 1971 that directly influenced Ethernet and later Wi-Fi).

In 1973, Vinton Cerf and Robert Kahn proposed a unifying internetworking architecture that evolved into the Transmission Control Program, the precursor to the Transmission Control Protocol (TCP). The first full TCP implementation was developed at Stanford in 1975. In November 1977, the TCP/Internet Protocol (TCP/IP) suite was successfully demonstrated in the landmark "three-network test," which interconnected ARPANET, SATNET, and the department's packet radio network (PRNET) using a common internetworking protocol.

This experiment showed that heterogeneous packet-switched networks could be combined under a common protocol suite, laying the groundwork for the modern Internet.

Flag Day. Adopted by the DoD in 1980, TCP/IP enabled the January 1, 1983, transition that established the modern Internet, with ARPANET splitting into MILNET (the DoD's military network) and a civilian research network.

By the late 1980s, the U.S. National Science Foundation (NSF) expanded access through NSFNET, leading to the retirement of ARPANET. When the NSF opened the network to commercial traffic in 1993, innovation surged. For two early examples, Mosaic and Netscape brought the Internet to homes and businesses worldwide, transforming communication, commerce, education, and social life.

On the Other End: In Pursuit of What Will Be – From a Couple of Loaner Phones to an Institutionalized Program

A newly activated command initially received, on loan, two government-issued BlackBerry cell phones from higher headquarters: one for the commander and one for the senior enlisted advisor. There was no local budget line, no property accountability, no lifecycle management, and no local information technology (IT) service and support requirements.

Soon after, the senior civilian executive requested and received a device, followed by the chief of staff. Around that time, the popular cell phone shifted from the BlackBerry to the iPhone, prompting the procurement of new iPhones to replace the government-issued BlackBerrys for the initial recipients.

As news spread throughout the command and more funds became readily available, deputy chiefs of staff requested and received iPhones. The expansion quickly cascaded down the chain of command: brigade commanders and their senior enlisted advisors, followed by battalion commanders and their counterparts. Next, executive officers, action officers, other senior personnel, and even those on temporary duty assignments.

The growing device inventory and expanding contracts required a formal command policy that specified eligibility by position. Unsurprisingly, this resulted in many requests for "exceptions to policy" from staff members who were not included.

Soon, tablets with cellular connectivity, such as iPads, were also issued. Many now carried two government-issued mobile devices—an iPhone and an iPad, each with a separate service plan. The increasingly widespread use of these devices led to requests for additional capabilities, including specific software applications and attachable card readers to support Common Access Card (CAC) authentication for online applications, thereby further increasing technical complexity.

Standard Operating Procedures (SOPs) needed to be written, staffed, and approved; then revised, restaffed, and reapproved to cover an increasingly larger number of areas, such as the "acceptable use" of government-issued mobile devices. For civilian employees, another concern arose: what counts as compensable overtime when messages are exchanged on these devices after duty hours?

Operating system updates needed to be monitored for compliance. Incidents of loss, theft, and damage required investigations. Monthly phone charges rapidly increased, prompting questions from higher HQ about the bills. Lifecycle management—covering procurement, configuration, issuance, upgrades, turn-in, deactivation, and disposal—became more complex.

Eventually, managing and monitoring mobile communications required a newly defined role with a dedicated IT specialist to work full-time managing the program. This led to the development of a local web application to track inventory and use within the command. Meanwhile, the complexities and costs continued to increase.

And this was in addition to managing approximately 9,000 IT assets already listed on the property book across the command's 35 geographically dispersed field offices.

What started as an ad hoc arrangement for two senior leaders quickly became an institutionalized responsibility. The command shifted from using a couple of loaner devices with no local IT service or support to a comprehensive, command-wide mobile communications program—with a dedicated budget, property accountability, lifecycle management, policies and procedures, additional staffing, specialized hardware and software, and a custom web application to automate management functions.

This is simply one brief, local example of expansion.

It isn't about criticizing efficiency or judgment. It's about promoting sustainability. When more resources are consistently available, organizations and their capabilities grow accordingly. In this case, we didn't cut back on anything else to pay for the rising costs of the new program because additional funding reliably covered the extra expenses. That is, we gained new capabilities while maintaining existing ones because we could increasingly afford to.

The same pattern appears on much larger scales—in enterprise software, hardware, and Army-wide IT services—where growth is often driven by increasing funding, staff, and management layers. In a plentiful environment, the department can always do more with more.

Of course, most of us don't have the option to do more with more.

Our growth comes from choices, not expansion. Meaningful change isn't about doing everything, chasing every opportunity, spending more, or borrowing against the future.

It is about committing ourselves to what we can maintain.

Unlike institutions that can often solve problems or explore possibilities by requesting more resources, we live in a world with limitations. Time, energy, attention, and money are finite. Each new commitment takes from what we already have. What begins as a good idea can quickly become an obligation we're responsible for maintaining long after the initial excitement fades.

Progress comes not from accumulation but from discipline: embracing challenges that stretch us without breaking us, developing ability without unnecessary burden, and choosing better—not simply more. Without self-control, efforts to grow can overwhelm us, leading to financial stress, diminished focus, and regret.

But this can be avoided. For sustainable self-improvement, the principle is simple: nothing too much.

Effective change comes from self-mastery—prioritizing needs over wants, aligning ambition with capacity, and improving deliberately with the resources we have today.

Notes and References

[1] Kurt Lewin, "Resolving Social Conflicts: Selected Papers on Group Dynamics," in *Resolving Social Conflicts and Field Theory in Social Science*, edited by Gertrude W. Lewin (1948; reprinted, Washington, D.C.: American Psychological Association, 2010), Kindle edition, loc. 4,233.

[2] Thomas H. Holmes and Richard H. Rahe, "The Social Readjustment Rating Scale," *Journal of Psychosomatic Research* 11, no. 2 (1967): 213–18, https://doi.org/10.1016/0022-3999(67)90010-4. The authors state that while some of these events are negative, others are socially desirable. They add that each of these life events, however, is either indicative of or requires a significant change in the individual's life. And, they say, "The emphasis is on change from the existing steady state and not on psychological meaning, emotion, or social desirability."

[3] Updated wording for select Life Events from the original 1967 research comes from: Denise Wallace, Nicholas R. Cooper, Alejandra Sel, and Riccardo Russo, "The Social Readjustment Rating Scale: Updated and Modernised," *PLoS ONE* 18, no. 12 (2023): e0295943, https://doi.org/10.1371/journal.pone.0295943.

[4] Marcus Aurelius, *Meditations*, translated by George Long, in *Great Books of the Western World*, edited by Robert Maynard Hutchins, vol. 12 (Chicago: Encyclopaedia Britannica, 1984), 283. (Original work written as a private journal ca. 180 C.E.).

[5] This leadership principle goes back to at least 1951. U.S. Department of the Army, *Field Manual 22-10: Leadership* (Washington, D.C.: U.S. Government Printing Office, 1951), 20, Digitized by the Internet Archive: accessed September 15, 2025, https://archive.org/details/FM22-10/page/n25/mode/2up.

[6] The other two are "Never too much" and "Give a pledge, and evil is nigh at hand." Plato, *Charmides*, translated by Benjamin Jowett, in *Great Books of the Western World*, edited by Robert Maynard Hutchins, vol. 7 (Chicago: Encyclopaedia Britannica, 1984), 7. (Plato's original work written ca. 380 BCE).

[7] Confucius, *Confucian Analects*, translated by James Legge, in *The Art of War and Other Classics of Eastern Thought* (New York: Barnes & Noble, 2014), 388. (Original work written in China ca. 500 BCE). The 2014 Barnes & Noble text of *Confucian Analects* is based on James Legge's first volume: Legge, James, translator. *The Chinese Classics. With a Translation, Critical and Exegetical Notes, Prolegomena, and Copious Indexes.* (London: Oxford University Press, 1893).

[8] Lao Tzu, *Tao Te Ching*, translated by James Legge, in *The Art of War and Other Classics of Eastern Thought* (New York: Barnes & Noble, 2014), 249. (Original work written ca. 6th century BCE). The 2014 Barnes & Noble text of the *Tao Te Ching* is

Notes and References

based on James Legge's translation: Legge, James, translator. *The Texts of Taoism*, Part 1. (London: Oxford University Press, 1891).

[9] Aristotle, *Nicomachean Ethics*, translated by W. D. Ross, in *Great Books of the Western World*, edited by Robert Maynard Hutchins, vol. 9, (Chicago: Encyclopaedia Britannica, 1984), 348–349. (Original work written ca. 4th century BCE).

[10] Will Durant, *The Story of Philosophy: The Lives and Opinions of the Greater Philosophers* (New York: Simon & Schuster, 1926), 87, Digitized by Internet Archive: accessed September 16, 2025, https://archive.org/details/in.ernet.dli.2015.264687/page/n103/mode/2up?q=%22excellence%2C+then%2C+is%22.

[11] Armed Services Vocational Aptitude Battery (ASVAB). "Home." Accessed November 13, 2025. https://www.officialasvab.com/.

[12] U.S. Army, *March2Success*, accessed November 12, 2025, https://www.march2success.com/.

[13] College Board. "SAT Participation for Class of 2025 Surpasses 2 Million Test Takers for First Time Since 2020." *College Board Newsroom*, September 30, 2025. https://newsroom.collegeboard.org/sat-participation-class-2025-surpasses-2-million-test-takers-first-time-2020.

[14] Khan Academy, *Digital SAT Practice*, accessed November 12, 2025, https://www.khanacademy.org/digital-sat.

[15] ACT, Inc., "Grad Class Database 2024," ACT Research, 2024, https://www.act.org/content/act/en/research/services-and-resources/data-and-visualization/grad-class-database-2024.html.

[16] ACT, Inc., "The ACT Test for Students," *ACT*, accessed January 9, 2026, https://www.act.org/content/act/en/products-and-services/the-act.html.

[17] CareerOneStop. "Skills Matcher." U.S. Department of Labor, Employment and Training Administration. 2025. https://www.careeronestop.org/Toolkit/Skills/skills-matcher.aspx.

[18] My Next Move. "My Next Move." National Center for O*NET Development, sponsored by the U.S. Department of Labor, Employment and Training Administration. 2025. https://www.mynextmove.org/.

[19] Open Psychometrics, "IPIP Big-Five Factor Markers," accessed December 8, 2025, https://openpsychometrics.org/tests/IPIP-BFFM/.

[20] MyersBriggsPersonalityTest.org, "Free Myers-Briggs Personality Test – Discover Your MBTI Type," accessed November 13, 2025, https://myersbriggspersonalitytest.org/.

[21] John L. Holland, *Making Vocational Choices: A Theory of Careers* (Englewood Cliffs, NJ: Prentice-Hall, 1973), Appendix C, Digitized by Internet Archive, https://archive.org/details/makingvocational00holl.

[22] National Center for O*NET Development. "O*NET Interest Profiler." O*NET Resource Center. Sponsored by the U.S. Department of Labor, Employment and Training Administration. Accessed December 2, 2025. https://www.onetcenter.org/IP.html

[23] Aptitudes, academic skills, and personality matter. For enlisted Soldiers, we become well aware of our aptitudes even before being inducted through the ASVAB. Our scores largely determine what jobs we're qualified for, and that remains true over an entire career. In Army leadership courses, we're also subject to mandatory personality assessments. In my case, I was required to take the Myers-Briggs Type Indicator (MBTI) assessment three times in three different settings over a many-year span, and each time I scored exactly the same: INTJ (introverted, intuitive, thinking, and judging). We were even required to post our type indicators on our desk nameplates in the classroom, so our classmates and instructors could see them clearly. To reemphasize, personality types are not good or bad, but tendencies to be aware of, and possibly adjust our actions and reactions accordingly.

[24] Francis Bacon, *Novum Organum*, in *Great Books of the Western World*, edited by Robert Maynard Hutchins, vol. 30 (Chicago: Encyclopacdia Britannica, 1984), 109–111. (Original work written 1620).

[25] Shunryu Suzuki, *Zen Mind, Beginner's Mind* (Boston: Shambhala Publications, 2020), Kindle edition, loc 228-236.

[26] Mark Muesse, *Practicing Mindfulness: An Introduction to Meditation* (Chantilly, VA: The Great Courses, 2011), 201–203.

[27] Plato, *Apology*, translated by Benjamin Jowett, in *Great Books of the Western World*, edited by Robert Maynard Hutchins, vol. 7 (Chicago: Encyclopaedia Britannica, 1984), 202. (Original work written ca. 390 BCE, depicting Socrates' defense at his trial in 399 BCE).

[28] Confucius. *Confucian Analects*, 376.

[29] Lao Tzu. *Tao Te Ching*, 266.

[30] Roland Huntford, *The Last Place on Earth: Scott and Amundsen's Race to the South Pole* (New York: Modern Library, 1999).

---

31 Craig R. Whitney, "Jeanne Calment, World's Elder, Dies at 122," *New York Times*, August 5, 1997, accessed February 7, 2025, https://www.ny-times.com/1997/08/05/world/jeanne-calment-world-s-elder-dies-at-122.html#

32 U.S. Department of the Army. *Field Manual 3-0: Operations (FM 3-0)*. Washington, DC: U.S. Department of the Army, March 2025. https://armypubs.army.mil/epubs/DR_pubs/DR_a/ARN43326-FM_3-0-000-WEB-1.pdf.

33 The Army refers to "Mission Command" as its approach to command and control. "Command and control is the exercise of authority and direction by a properly designated commander over assigned and attached forces in the accomplishment of mission (JP 1). Command and control (also known as C2) is fundamental to the art and science of warfare. No single activity in operations is more important than command and control." U.S. Department of the Army, *Army Doctrine Publication 6-0: Mission Command.* (Washington, DC: Headquarters, Department of the Army, July 2019), 1–16. https://armypubs.army.mil/epubs/DR_pubs/DR_a/ARN34403-ADP_6-0-000-WEB-3.pdf.

34 Stephen R. Covey, *The 7 Habits of Highly Effective People: Powerful Lessons in Personal Change*, 25th Anniversary ed. (New York: Simon & Schuster, 2004), 88–100.

35 Julian B. Rotter, "Generalized Expectancies for Internal Versus External Control of Reinforcement." *Psychological Monographs: General and Applied* 80, no. 1 (1966): 1-28. https://doi.org/10.1037/h0092976

36 Alcoholics Anonymous. "M-2 Twelve and Twelve Wallet Card." Accessed March 11, 2025. https://www.aa.org/m-2-twelve-and-twelve-wallet-card For AA's historical review of the prayer, see "SMF-129 Origin of the Serenity Prayer: A Historical Paper" at: https://www.aa.org/origin-serenity-prayer-historical-paper.

37 Marcus Aurelius, *Meditations*, 302.

38 Marcus Aurelius, *Meditations*, 289.

39 Epictetus, *The Discourses of Epictetus*, translated by George Long, in *Great Books of the Western World*, edited by Robert Maynard Hutchins, vol. 12 (Chicago: Encyclopaedia Britannica, 1984), 105.

40 Epictetus, *The Enchiridion*, translated by George Long (Mineola, NY: Dover Publications, 2004), Kindle edition, locs. 44–56.

41 Mark Muesse, *Practicing Mindfulness: An Introduction to Meditation*, 146.

[42] Abraham Lincoln, *Address before the Wisconsin State Agricultural Society, Milwaukee, Wisconsin*, September 30, 1859, in *Collected Works of Abraham Lincoln. Volume 3 [Aug. 21, 1858–Mar. 4, 1860]*, University of Michigan Library Digital Collections, accessed March 14, 2025, https://quod.lib.umich.edu/l/lincoln/lincoln3/1:144?rgn=div1;view=fulltext

[43] *The Teaching of Buddha*, 1013th rev. ed. (Tokyo: Bukkyo Dendo Kyokai [Society for the Promotion of Buddhism], 2000), 588.

[44] I learned of wu-wei as an Army student studying the theory of war and military strategy. Applying wu-wei in the conduct of war, when it's necessary to go to war, we use only the power needed to achieve our goals, and not more than that. If we must go to war, it's preferable to conduct it with the fewest resources and avoid loss of life through skillful generalship rather than relying on brute force.

[45] Lao Tzu. *Tao Te Ching*, 254.

[46] Marcus Aurelius. *Meditations*, 299.

[47] Lao Tzu. *Tao Te Ching*, 263. The Chinese word "li" in this passage refers to the Chinese mile, a traditional unit of measurement for distance.

[48] The dates and core content presented here come from Britannica, unless otherwise noted. For Britannica information, see https://www.britannica.com/.

[49] Abraham H. Maslow, *A Theory of Human Motivation* (New York: Start Publishing LLC, 2012), Kindle edition, loc. 195. (Original work written in 1943).

[50] Viktor Frankl, *Man's Search for Meaning*. Translated by Ilse Lasch. Foreword by Harold S. Kushner. Afterword by William J. Winslade. (Boston: Beacon Press, 2014), 92. His original work was published in German in 1946, under the title *A Psychologist Experiences the Concentration Camp*.

[51] Carl Jung, *Memories, Dreams, Reflections* (New York: Crown Publishing Group/Random House, 1963), 390, Digitized by the Internet Archive: accessed September 18, 2025: https://archive.org/details/MemoriesDreamsReflectionsCarlJung_201811/page/n389/mode/2up?q=%22human+existence%22

[52] Alfred Adler, *What Life Should Mean to You* (London: George Allen & Unwin Ltd, 1932), 3, 9, Digitized by the Internet Archive: accessed September 18, 2025, https://archive.org/details/in.ernet.dli.2015.234444/mode/2up

[53] Sigmund Freud, *Civilization and Its Discontents*, translated by Joan Riviere, in *Great Books of the Western World*, edited by Robert Maynard Hutchins, vol. 54 (Chicago: Encyclopædia Britannica, 1984), 771. (Original work written in 1929).

---

[54] Friedrich Nietzsche, *The Twilight of the Idols: Or, How to Philosophise with the Hammer*. Translated by Anthony M. Ludovici. (London: George Allen & Unwin Ltd, 1927), Digitized by the Internet Archive: accessed September 19, 2025, https://archive.org/details/dli.ministry.06904/page/1/mode/2up. (Original work written in German in 1888).

[55] Viktor Frankl, *Man's Search for Meaning*, 72.

[56] Jocelyn Hutchinson, "Ikigai," *Research Starters – Religion and Philosophy*, EBSCO, 2024, https://www.ebsco.com/research-starters/religion-and-philosophy/ikigai.

[57] Héctor García and Francesc Miralles, *Ikigai: The Japanese Secret to a Long and Happy Life*, translated by Heather Cleary (New York: Penguin Books, 2016), 9.

[58] Aristotle, *Nicomachean Ethics*, 343.

[59] The dates and summarized content in this section are derived from Encyclopedia Britannica online: https://www.britannica.com/.

[60] Erik H. Erikson, *Childhood and Society* (New York: W. W. Norton & Company, 1950), 231, Digitized by the Internet Archive, accessed October 27, 2025, https://archive.org/details/dli.ernet.19961/page/231/mode/2up.

[61] Milton Rokeach, *The Nature of Human Values* (New York: Free Press, 1973).

[62] Richard P. Feynman, "Cargo Cult Science," *Engineering and Science* 37, no. 7 (June 1974): 12, https://calteches.library.caltech.edu/51/. This quote comes from *Some remarks on science, pseudoscience, and learning how to not fool yourself* – delivered at Caltech's 1974 commencement address.

[63] Warren E. Buffett, Chairman's Letter – 1996, Berkshire Hathaway Inc., published 1997, accessed March 14, 2025, https://berkshirehathaway.com/letters/1996.html.

[64] René Descartes, *Discourse on the Method of Rightly Conducting the Reason*, translated by E. S. Haldane and G. R. T. Ross, in *Great Books of the Western World*, edited by Robert Maynard Hutchins, vol. 31 (Chicago: Encyclopaedia Britannica, 1984), 47. (Original work written 1637).

[65] Confucius. *Confucian Analects*, 376.

[66] The Buddha, *Kalama Sutta (Kesamutta Sutta)* (Singapore: Singapore Buddhist Meditation Center, 1999), 1, accessed March 17, 2025, Digitized by Internet Archive, https://ia803404.us.archive.org/13/items/kalama-sutta/Kalama%20Sutta.pdf.

---

[67] American Academy of Sleep Medicine and Sleep Research Society, *Joint Consensus Statement: Recommended Amount of Sleep for a Healthy Adult* (2015), accessed October 15, 2025, https://aasm.org/resources/pdf/pressroom/adult-sleep-duration-consensus.pdf.

[68] Defense Technical Information Center. *DTIC.* Accessed December 13, 2025. https://discover.dtic.mil/.

[69] Department of the Army, *ADP 1-01: Doctrine Primer* (Washington, DC: Headquarters, Department of the Army, July 2019), 2-3 to 2-4, accessed December 22, 2025, https://armypubs.army.mil/epubs/DR_pubs/DR_a/pdf/web/ARN18138_ADP%201-01%20FINAL%20WEB.pdf.

[70] Army Publishing Directorate. *Army Publishing Directorate.* Accessed December 12, 2025. https://armypubs.army.mil/.

[71] Hillel the Elder, *Pirkei Avot* 1:14, in *Mishnah*, accessed October 30, 2025, https://www.sefaria.org/Pirkei_Avot.1.14.

[72] National Library of Medicine. *MedlinePlus – Health Information from the National Library of Medicine.* U.S. National Institutes of Health. Accessed March 17, 2025. https://medlineplus.gov

[73] U.S. Army Europe and Center of Military History, *"Countdown to 75: US Army Europe and Post-Cold War,"* Army.mil, May 9, 2017, https://www.army.mil/article/187118/countdown_to_75_us_army_europe_and_post_cold_war.

[74] We'll revisit the failure of this program in *Phase Two*, where we'll explore how to choose effective approaches for pursuing change. For now, the Defense Integrated Military Human Resources System (DIMHRS) serves as a classic example of how large government programs can fail spectacularly, despite the time, effort, and money invested. Such large-scale failures often stem from unresolved factors that are difficult to identify, and money is often not among them.

In this case, the Government Accountability Office (GAO) conducted extensive investigations to assess the program's status. For instance, see the September 2008 report (GAO-08-927R), available at https://www.gao.gov/products/gao-08-927r, that discusses some concerns we raised for the Army. Ultimately, after ten years of effort, the program was canceled in February 2010.

[75] The 2005 Base Realignment and Closure (BRAC) round coordinated the relocation of more than 123,000 people, making it far more extensive than previous rounds. This effort earned it the title "the mother of all BRACs." See Government Accountability Office, *Military Base Realignments and Closures: Key Factors Contribute to Challenges in Implementing Closure and Realignment Recommendations,* GAO-12-513T

(Washington, DC: Government Accountability Office, 2012), https://www.gao.gov/products/gao-12-513t.

It also affected over 800 locations, 24 major closures, 24 major realignments, and 765 lesser actions. See: Department of Defense. *Report on 2005 Defense Base Closure and Realignment Implementation, Volume I.* Washington, DC: Department of Defense, June 2008. Accessed November 21, 2025, https://media.defense.gov/2022/Jun/08/2003014185/-1/-1/0/2008_SECTION_2907_REPORT.PDF.

[76] Paul G. Nyce, *UNIVAC I Becomes the First Commercial Electronic Computer*, EBSCO Research Starters, 2023, https://www.ebsco.com/research-starters/history/univac-i-becomes-first-commercial-electronic-computer.

[77] The Aerospace Corporation, *Brief History of GPS*, The Aerospace Corporation, accessed December 11, 2025, https://aerospace.org/article/brief-history-gps.

[78] Kevin Featherly, *ARPANET*, Encyclopedia Britannica, November 4, 2025, https://www.britannica.com/topic/ARPANET.

[79] Robert Kahn, Michael Aaron Dennis, *Internet. Encyclopedia Britannica*, November 29, 2025. https://www.britannica.com/technology/Internet.